THE BIG BOOK OF

HACKS

FOR

MINECRAFTERS

THE BIG BOOK OF
HACKS
FOR
MINECRAFTERS

THE UNOFFICIAL GUIDE TO TIPS AND TRICKS THAT OTHER GUIDES WON'T TEACH YOU

MEGAN MILLER

Sky Pony Press
New York

Copyright © 2015 by Hollan Publishing, Inc.

Minecraft® is a registered trademark of Notch Development AB

The Minecraft game is copyright © Mojang AB

Visit our website at www.skyponypress.com.

10 9 8 7 6 5 4 3 2

Manufactured in the United States, October 2015
This product conforms to CPSIA 2008

Library of Congress Cataloging-in-Publication Data is available on file.

Cover design by Owen Corrigan

TABLE OF CONTENTS

Hacks for Minecrafters: Combat Edition

HACKS

FOR

MINECRAFTERS

INTRODUCTION

You're a miner! You've mined for diamonds, killed a couple or a million zombies, and know not to dig straight up or straight down! Now what? Plenty. Minecraft is a constantly evolving sandbox game. This means the developers of the game add new things each year and there are many ways to play. For version 1.8, Minecraft added ocean monuments, new blocks like red sandstone and prismarine, banners, rabbits, updated villagers and enchanting, and much more. You can expect this game to grow and change as you learn, so there are always new things to explore and experiment with.

And each year, thousands of players find new tricks to get things done better, faster, or with more fun. This book will show you lots of ways to help your game, whether you like to fight zombies or build castles, including:

- how to save a village from a siege of zombies

- what to do first to defeat the Ender Dragon

- how to find one of your world's three strongholds

- how to make automatic sliding doors using pistons and redstone

- how to move between Creative and Survival modes using cheats

NOTE: The tips in this book are based on Minecraft 1.8.1, PC version, so if you are playing a different version or are playing on a console, you may find that some features work a little differently.

CHAPTER 1

PLAYING YOUR WAY

Minecraft is a sandbox game, which means there aren't any rules for how you play. In a sandbox, you can build a sand-castle, dig a road, or throw a bunch of sand around. In Mine-craft, you can build a massive railway system, make friends with wolves and ocelots, explore the oceans, or kill an army of zombies. Or do it all. There's no goal that you must achieve, but if you like goals, Minecraft has a few you can set your sights on. It's up to you to decide how to play, and you can mix it up any way you want to.

Minecraft Game Modes

Minecraft has different game modes you choose at the start. They are geared to the different types of gameplay.

- **Survival and Hardcore:** In Survival mode you have to find food and shelter, and you can be killed. If you are killed, you respawn at your starting point without your inventory. (Your inventory items stay at your death scene for five minutes before they despawn—so you do have a chance to get them back.) There are four difficulty levels: Peaceful (no mobs), Easy (mobs do less damage), Normal (mobs do normal damage), and Hard (mobs do more damage and you can die from hunger). In Hardcore mode, you play at Hard difficulty, you can't have cheats, and your world is deleted if you are killed!

In Hard difficulty, mobs are more likely to spawn with weapons, armor, and enchantments, and they will cause you more damage.

- **Adventure:** Adventure mode is like Survival, except you can't interact with many blocks. It is designed for playing on adventure maps.

- **Creative:** Creative mode is perfect for building. You can fly around, and you have access to all the blocks. Your inventory changes to an item selection screen with a search page. To fly, press the spacebar twice. To go higher, press the spacebar again. To descend, press Shift.

- **Changing Mode:** To change game mode while you are playing, create your world with cheats on. Then, to change mode, open the chat window by pressing T and type the following:

- For Survival mode: /gamemode 0 (or /gamemode s or /gamemode survival)

- For Creative mode: /gamemode 1 (or /gamemode c or/gamemode creative)

- For Adventure mode: /gamemode 2, (or /gamemode a or /gamemode adventure)

- For Spectator mode: /gamemode 3 (or /gamemode sp or /gamemode spectator)

In Creative mode you can fly around, which is a huge help if you're building a tower in sky!

Want Some Goals?

If you are goal-oriented, you can play that way, too. Minecraft has a series of about thirty achievements you can use as quests. Accomplish one and make your way to the next. These can also guide you through the Minecraft survival skills. They start off very simple, and you have probably already accomplished many. The first is Taking Inventory, which you achieve by pressing E. To see what you've accomplished so far, and what's next, press Escape to open the Options screen and then click Achievements. (Click the Statistics button to see how many creepers you've killed, fish you've caught, blocks you've mined, and more.)

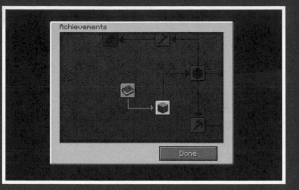

If you like playing with goals, use your achievement screen for new tasks.

You can track everything you've accomplished in your statistics screen, from how much iron you've mined to how many zombies you've killed.

There's also a way to "win" at Minecraft in a special final battle against the Ender Dragon in a realm called the End. It's difficult to get there, because to prepare you must learn how to use potions, kill Endermen, and survive the Nether to gather essential items.

Making the Most out of Minecraft

Don't Stress Out

You're going to die. Unless you are in Creative mode, something will get you at some point. Even in Peaceful mode, it might be a fall into a lava pool. But that is part of the game. Prepare for this as best you can by storing your goods in chests you can find later and, of course, remembering where your chests and home are.

Switch It Up

If you need a break from the mobs for a bit, switch to Peaceful mode. To change the difficulty level in Survival, press Escape on your keyboard and change the options under Difficulty.

If you enabled cheats when you created your world, you can type commands in the chat window. Press t to open the window, and then type a slash and your command. /time set day changes the game to daytime.

Use Cheats Wisely

Using cheats, or commands, can make survival game play feel less rewarding. But if you are playing in Creative mode and need to work free of mob attacks, you may want to also use commands. To use commands you must create your world with Cheats on. Then you can open up the chat window by pressing T. (The chat window only works for chatting if you are in multiplayer.) You type your command into the chat window, preceded by a slash. (You can also open up the chat window by typing the initial slash of the command.) So to change to Creative mode, type **/gamemode c**. To switch back to Survival mode, type **/gamemode s**. You can also change your difficulty level by typing **/difficulty 0** (for Peaceful) through **/difficulty 3** (Hard). Another popular cheat is to grant one-self experience, through **/xp X** (where X is the number of experience points). You can teleport anywhere, if you know your coordinates, with **/tp X Y Z**. For a list of available commands, type **/help**.

Worlds and Seeds

If you just like to explore worlds, or if you're having a hard time finding structures like jungle temples, you can play in worlds other players have found. Each world is started with a "seed." When Minecraft creates a world, it generates a random number called a seed to spawn the world. You can see your world's seed by typing **/seed** in the chat window.

You can visit a world someone else found by entering the seed number for that world in your world's options screen.

You can also enter your own random number or sequence of characters in the More World Options screen, under Seed for the World Generator. Users share the seeds they have used on-line, at websites like minecraft-seeds.net. Find a world whose description you like at one of these sites, make sure the world was created using the same game version you are using, and type the seed for that world into your World Options screen. You can enter letters for a seed number, too. See what world is generated when you type in your own name! You can also change the basic type of world by clicking the World Type button:

- Superflat: This is a flat world with one grass block on top of two dirt blocks and one layer of bedrock. You can customize the layers and depths using the Customize button, or you can use a preset type of superflat world.

- Large biomes: This makes the biomes sixteen times bigger.

- Amplified: This makes mountains even taller, but this could slow down your computer game.

Manage Your Inventory

For many players, it can be much easier and faster to use shortcuts to move stuff between your inventory and other containers and slots.

- Press 1 through 9 to access the items in your hotbar.

To access items in your hotbar quickly, type the number for that slot, from 1 to 9 (left to right).

- Press Shift and click to move a stack between your inventory and hotbar or between a container with an inventory and your hotbar/inventory.

- Shift-click armor to have it go straight into the right armor slots.

- Move items between the inventory and a specific slot in your hotbar by hovering over the item or blank slot in the inventory and pressing the number for that slot, from 0 to 9.

- If your furnace is open, Shift-clicking an item like a raw pork chop or coal will move it to the right slot.

- Right-click to pick up half a stack.

- Double-click an item to pick up as many as a full stack (64) as available in your inventory.

- To move as many items of one kind as you can from your inventory to a chest, pick up any item, press Shift, and double-click the item you want to move.

- Right-click when you are holding a stack to drop just one item from it.

- When you're crafting, you can right-click and drag over the slots to drop one item at a time from your stack into each slot. You can do this multiple times to keep adding an item to each slot.

- To craft as many items as possible from stacked craft slots, press Shift-click in the crafted item slot.

Manage Your Tools

Keep track of the damage your tools and weapons are taking, and repair them before they are broken. Craft one used tool with another tool of the same kind. As long as the total damage between the two is more than 5 percent, this gives you even more durability than using each tool separately.

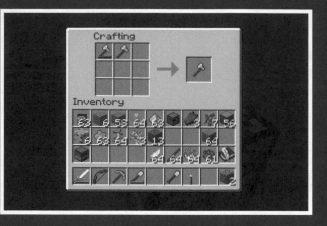

Repair your damaged tools by combining them with a new one. This gives them extra durability.

Modding Your Game

Minecraft was designed to allow other people to modify it. There are three main ways to customize your game. However, it is very easy to download an application or file that can damage your game or your computer. We recommend that if you do want to modify your game, you enlist the help of a parent or a friend who has already successfully done this. You need to make sure that any new files or applications you use are compatible with the exact version of the game you are playing; make backups of your game files before making any changes, and check for viruses!

- **Skins:** You can change the way your player character looks by uploading an image file, called a skin. You can find skins online or create your own using a skin editor. An easy way to change your skin is to download a skin that you like at a Minecraft skins website, like minecraftskins.com. Log in to your account at minecraft.net and go to your profile page. Click Browse to locate the new file on your computer and then Upload to change your skin.

A skin is a small image file that is used to show what your character looks like. Many games, including Minecraft, let you change your skin. This is a dragon found at minecraftskins.com.

- **Resource and texture packs**: These are sets of files that replace game resources like sounds, textures (image files) that make blocks look the way they do, and music. They don't change the basic way the game plays.

- **Mods:** Mods are programs you download that change something about the way the game operates. For example, one mod may add tons of new creatures to your game, from bunnies to werewolves, and another may add new fantastical plants.

Keep Learning!

Millions of people, adults and kids, play Minecraft. They are talking about Minecraft online, playing together in multiplayer games, and making videos and tutorials. Some of the best places to learn about Minecraft are from YouTube videos and at the Minecraft wiki at minecraft.gamepedia.com.

CHAPTER 2

NAVIGATING YOUR WORLD

Your Minecraft world is enormous. It has changing land-scapes, called biomes, changing weather, and an endless numbers of caverns, lakes, seas, and lands. The downside is, there are no signs or guideposts. It is very easy to travel fast, chase a pig, flee from a creeper, get turned around, and get lost.

So a key strategy in Minecraft is to always know where you are, where home is, and how to get back. You probably have already learned to make a pillar beacon at your base. This can help to orient you if you are not too far away, but it won't help if you are very far away from home or if tall mountains are in the way. So when you build your pillar beacon, be sure it is higher than nearby mountains. Add more than one torch at the top to help blaze up the sky at night!

When you build a pillar beacon, make sure it is taller than surrounding mountains and brightly lit.

Compasses and maps may seem like the answer, but a compass always points to your original spawn point. If you've reset your spawn point by sleeping in a bed somewhere else, the compass can't help. Maps work great, but to cover a large area you will need a set of large maps. To craft a large map or a zoomed out map, use a map in the crafting area center surrounded by eight papers. You can do this four times to create a map that is sixteen times as big as the original map size.

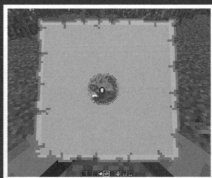

You can create four bigger sizes of a map from your first map.

A quick way to track your path as you go is to punch out the center sections of trees as you pass (if you are in a forest).

For a fast trail in a forest, punch out the centers of trees.

Or, if you are in a desert area, drop blocks of dirt (they'll stand out!). In a non-desert area, drop blocks of sand. You can use other blocks, just make sure they are easily noticeable in the landscape.

Leave blocks as breadcrumbs on your way.

If you're looking for or exploring interesting caves and ravines during your travels, mark them as you go. Use one type of marker to say, "Explore here!" and another to say, "Already explored." For a really important marker that you want to be able to spot easily, make a mini-tower with a torch.

You can use your own system and ideas for markers. This ravine has been marked with sand and red wool to show it's been explored.

Using X and Z to Mark the Spot

Probably the best way to keep track of your home, and where you are at any time, is to use Minecraft's location coordinates, which you find by opening the Debug screen. To open the Debug screen, press F3 (or on some laptops, Fn+F3. Fn is the Function key). The Debug screen shows information about things like chunks (the sixteen-block sections of world that the Minecraft programming manages) and memory. The most important information for you is the X, Y, Z, and F numbers, which are near the bottom of the screen. With coordinates, the "center" of the world is at 0, 0, 0.

Listed toward the bottom of the debug screen are the X, Y, Z coordinates and the direction you are facing in (F).

X: Shows where you are along an east-west line. Negative numbers show you are west of 0, 0.

Z: Shows where you are along a north-south line. Negative numbers show you are north of 0, 0.

Y: Shows the altitude or how high you are, from down in the mines (near 0) to mountains.

F: Shows you what direction you are facing—east, west, north, or south.

The important ones to record your location are the X and Z numbers. Keep a notebook (in the real world) to mark down the coordinates for home and other important places you find, like villages, temples, and abandoned mineshafts you want to explore. You could also keep a note on signs in your inventory, but these will be lost if you are killed.

Getting Home by Numbers

When you get lost and you have your home base coordinates noted down somewhere, you can open up the Debug screen, look at your current X and Z position, and figure out what direction you need to go. It can be easiest to travel in one direction at a time, because the numbers on the Debug screen change very quickly, and it is hard to keep track of more than one number at a time. For example, if you need to go further east, concentrate on making sure you are facing east with the F number and then move in that direction. Keep looking at the screen to make sure that the X numbers are increasing (going further east) in your Debug screen. Of course, you may need to detour to avoid mountains or lakes!

More Navigating Tips

- Clouds always travel west, so if you can't see the sun, you can tell the direction by the clouds.

- Bring a map underground—it will show if there is lava, sand, or water above you if you need to dig up.

- To mark your way, you can also remove the leaves from trees in your path, use dyed wool blocks, or use Jack o'Lanterns. You can use the face on the Jack o'Lantern to point the right direction!

When you place a Jack o'Lantern, its face is toward you. If you keep the faces all the same direction, this can help point you in the right direction.

- If you are traveling slowly, you could dig out a trench as you go. You can use cobblestone or other blocks later to make it into a path.

Traveling by Boat

In addition to traveling by foot and by horse, you can travel long distances by sea pretty fast, and if you have a river system, that is a good way to explore quickly. If you hold a zoomed-out map, you can fill out a lot pretty quickly. However, boats break pretty easily. If you are planning a voyage, bring a small stack of boats. If the one you are in is destroyed, get out another boat and right-click into it.

Exploring by boat.

To make a boat, you need five blocks of wood planks. Place your boat by right-clicking on the water. Enter your boat by right-clicking it, and leave it by pressing the sneak key (the Shift key). To drive your boat, use the W key to move forward and your crosshairs to turn left and right. You can use the S key to move back, but the boat will turn underneath you to face the opposite direction. Boats are easily damaged by hitting other blocks and lily, and if damaged enough will break up.

More Boat Tips

- You can even place your boat on land and drive it. But you will go pretty slowly!

- Your hunger bar stays at the same level when you travel by boat.

- Break a boat to get it back into inventory.

- If you are in a boat, you are protected from hostile land mobs.

CHAPTER 3

EXPLORING

Along with mining for rare ores and crafting cool objects, exploring your world is a major Minecraft activity. It's how you find rare plants, villagers to trade with, horses to tame, and temples to loot! One thing to know is what you can expect in all the different landscapes, or biomes, in Minecraft. You'll only find a jungle temple in the jungle, of course, but what can you find in the cold, snowy areas? Keep an eye out as you explore. You can use the Debug screen to find out exactly what biome you are in.

In the snowy biomes, the ones with spruce and oak trees (called "Taiga"), you can find wolves. Taiga is a name for coniferous northern forests; conifers have needle leaves. Cold biomes are rockier and have more trees than the snowy biomes. Wolves are more common in the cold Taiga biomes. In the medium and lush biomes you find plains,

To find what biome you are in, press F3 (or Fn + F3) to open the Debug screen and look for the entry "Biome". This is the Savanna biome.

forests, swamplands, rivers, mushroom islands, beaches, and jungles. There are more ponds, rivers, and plants. Witch's huts are found in swamplands, and jungles are home to ocelots, cocoa beans, wild melons, and jungle temples. Like the cold biomes, the dry or warm biomes have less animal and plant life. There are deserts with cactus, savannahs with acacia trees, and mesas with dry clay. You find villages in plains, deserts, and savannahs.

As you explore, look out for caves, ravines, villages, desert temples, jungle temples, and ocean monuments, as these are great places to find rare items that you cannot mine or craft.

Exploring Caves

If you are exploring a cave system, it's especially easy to get turned around because it all kind of looks the same. A very simple way to mark your way is this: put torches on the right side of the cave wall, and only the right side, as you explore.

An easy way to keep track of your steps is by placing torches only on your right. Then to exit, make sure your placed torches are on your left. Mark any forks with a double torch showing the way back out.

When you retrace your steps back to the entrance, all you do is keep those torches to your left side. (You can do the opposite, too; just keep to the same tactic always.) When you use this tactic, be careful when you hit a fork. You need make sure to mark *which* fork leads back toward the entrance. An easy way to do this is just leave two torches, one on top of the other.

When you reach a fork, use two torches to mark which way leads you back to the cave entrance.

If you are finished exploring a section, mark it done.

Use signs to leave notes for yourself ("Obsidian this way!" "Exit here!"). Use dashes and the greater than (>) sign to make arrows.

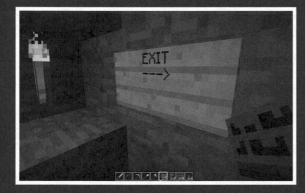

Use signs to show important finds and the exit

You can sometimes find a dungeon in a cave—these are cobblestone and mossy rooms that hold a chest. But watch out: there's almost always a mob spawner you will have to disarm!

Dungeons usually have chests with rare items—and a spawner!

Abandoned Mineshafts

Abandoned mineshafts are created automatically with each new world. They are underground mazes of tunnels and shafts, partly broken up but lined and loaded with wood, rails, fencing, and cobwebs, ready to loot. You can also find chests that hold a few rare items like enchanted books and saddles, seeds, and often bread. There are torches already lit in these mineshafts, so there are fewer mobs. Of course, they do come with a downside—cave spider spawners. These are surrounded by thick layers of cobwebs. Cobwebs slow you down, but not the cave spiders! Cave spiders are smaller than regular spiders, so they can get through a 1×1 hole. Be warned!

You'll know you've found an abandoned mineshaft when you spot the wooden beams, posts, and tracks. Inside you'll find rails, ore, chests, and more to harvest.

Use shears or a sword to collect cobwebs. You can also use flint and steel to light cobwebs on fire, and you may kill a couple cave spiders along with that! Kill cave spiders with a bow or sword, and take a pickaxe to destroy the spawner. If you are bitten by a spider, eat a golden apple or drink milk to heal. If part of a mineshaft is blocked by water or lava flow, see if there is any easy way to block that flow with cobblestone so you can keep exploring.

Despite the hazards, abandoned mineshafts are a treasure trove of loot. The easiest way to go looking for them is to look along the inside walls of ravines for the signs of a mineshaft below— wooden bridges crossing the ravine.

Getting Down a Ravine

There are several ways to get down a ravine. Drop blocks of sand or dirt at the edge, letting them drop all the way down. Once the stack is up to your level, jump on and dig down. Another way to get to the bottom of a ravine fast is to make a waterfall. A block or two from the edge of a ravine, pour some water so it flows into the ravine. Make sure that the wall you are pouring against goes straight down, and that there is a puddle of water at the bottom for you to land in. Step into the waterfall and let it carry you down. You can also swim back up a waterfall. Or, if you have a little time, just make steps down the side of the ravine. Depending on how the wall curves, you may need to dig in a little to turn a corner every once in a while.

One way to get down a steep cliff is to pour water over the side. Make sure the cliff edge is straight and the water ends in a puddle for you to land in.

Desert temples are another great source of loot, but you have to avoid or defuse the explosive TNT trap inside. When you enter through the main doors, there is an orange and blue wool block pattern in the floor. This hides a very deep chamber beneath, with a pressure plate connected to nine TNT blocks beneath the floor.

A desert temple.

At the edges of this hidden chamber are four chests holding rare and valuable loot such as diamonds, emeralds, enchanted books, and saddles.

Inside the temple is a floor that hides a chamber. In the chamber are four treasure chests, booby trapped to a pressure plate. If you touch the pressure plate, nine blocks of TNT will explode!

You need to get down to the bottom of this chamber without touching the pressure plate. Some people make a waterfall to swim down, but this gets you pretty close to the pressure plate. A safer way is to dig a staircase down on the side or toward the chamber. Then you can break the pressure plate, loot the chests, and collect the TNT and the chests.

Ocean Monuments

You'll find ocean monuments only in deep ocean. They are dark, large, mazelike structures made from rare blocks like prismarine, dark prismarine, and ocean lanterns. They hold a hidden treasure in their central room: 8 gold blocks wrapped in dark prismarine. You will also find the fierce ocean mobs—the guardian and the mightier elder guardian—that protect the monument from you! To fight these you will definitely need potions, enchantments, and a very sharp sword. If an ocean monument is near land, you could try tunneling to it. Find the coordinates of the center of the monument as you boat over. Then tunnel from land to the bottom center of the monument. It is easier to fight guardians inside the monument, because it is harder for them to dart away.

The top of an ocean monument is close to the surface, so watch out for rectangular shapes in the deep ocean biome.

Jungle Temples

Like desert temples, jungle temples have both loot and booby traps. The jungle temple has two chests. On one side of the temple is a lever puzzle you must solve to open up the hole to one chest. There are three levers, and you must play with these to see what order of up and down will reveal the chest.

Like desert temples, jungle temples have both loot and booby traps. The jungle temple has two chests. On one side of the temple is a lever puzzle you must solve to open up the hole to one chest. There are three levers, and you must play with these to see what order of up and down will reveal the chest.

Go down the main stairs in a jungle temple to find the puzzle and the booby traps. On one side of the stairs is a puzzle of three levers.

On the other side of the temple, there is a corridor that is booby trapped with trip wires. If you set off the trip wires, this will trigger a dispenser that will fire arrows right at you! Go in the temple front doors—there will be a level above and below you. Below you on one side of the stairs are the three levers; on the other side is the booby-trapped hallway.

The trip wire is very hard to see. It is a little line that crosses across the floor of the hall. It's easier to spot the trip wire hooks on the sides of the corridor. Use a pickaxe to break up the trip wire hooks and disarm the trip wire. You can also cut the trip wire with shears. At the end of the corridor is the dispenser in the wall, covered in vines, which you can right click to loot the arrows. Be careful—a little further along is another trip wire in front of another dispenser, guarding a chest. Disarm the trip wire in the same way!

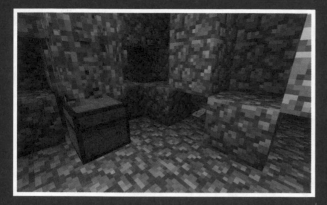

Once you get past the first set of trip wires in the jungle temple, there is another set. The trip wire hook is to the right, and the arrow dispenser is hidden in vines above the chest.

For the lever puzzle, the combination depends on whether the levers are to the right or the left of the stairs back up. On the right of the stairs, click the furthest right lever, the furthest left lever, then the middle. Then, flick the middle one up, then the left, then the right. For levers that are to the left of the stairs, flip down the left, right, then middle, and flip up the middle, right, and left. Go up the stairs. A hole has opened in the floor. Dig down to get to that area to find the second chest! Along with the chest treasure, collect all the special blocks used in making the traps and levers work: trip wire, dispensers, pistons, redstone, and redstone repeater.

More Exploring Tips

- Always carry a full stack of torches so you can light passageways and caves as you go to prevent mobs from spawning.
- Ladders are a great way to travel up and down fast. You can use the sneak key (Shift key) to pause while you're on a ladder.
- At the edge of a cliff or ravine, use the sneak key. This lets you move very slowly a little distance over the edge so you can peer below. You can also use this to help you build a bridge right in front of you, over lava pools, deep holes, and ravines.

CHAPTER 4

MINING

If you're playing Minecraft, then you've probably logged quite a few hours hacking into the ground and caves. You've amassed a good loot of coal, iron, and even diamonds and redstone. But getting all this great loot out of the ground takes some time, especially if you haven't found enough diamonds for making the strongest pickaxe. Over the years, miners of the world have debated what the best tactics are for spending the least amount of time and getting the most amount of stuff. Here are some of the best tactics to take you to the top of the leaderboard in mining.

Plan Your Trip!

If you're going mining, take enough essentials to last. At the very least you'll want a good stack of torches, a crafting table, several pickaxes and shovels, and plenty of food. There's not much food underground, or much wood (unless you run into an abandoned mineshaft!), so bring a stack of wood blocks and plenty of munchies.

The Safest Mining

Want to avoid the skeletons and cave spiders but don't want to change to Peaceful mode? Since mobs spawn in the dark, control the dark. Start mining from scratch in your own protected home, and make sure you are well lit all the way down. If you come across the opening to a dark cave, block it off. Mark the opening somehow, in case you want to explore later. You could even put a door there!

To mine monster-free, mine from home and keep well lit all the way!

Choose Your Tools

Remember to dig with the right tools, using the most durable tool you have. Use the pickaxe for ore and cobblestone and use a shovel for dirt, gravel, and sand. Keep your tools in the same spot on your hotbar, so that you can always type a 1, for example, to get your pickaxe. This makes switching between tools easy and fast.

If you keep the same tools in the same slots in your hotbar and type the number of the slot (1–9), you can be very quick at changing between tools (and weapons!).

Level 11

All the different types of ore—from charcoal to diamond—are found between different levels in the ground. The bottom level in the Overworld, level 0, is bedrock. Bedrock is tough—you can't get through it, you can't mine it, and it's indestructible. It's what separates the Overworld from the Nether.

The bottom layer of the Overworld is bedrock. It's at layer 0, and you can't mine through it.

The next block up from bedrock is level 1, then level 2, and so forth. You can find diamond between levels 1 and 15, emerald between 4 and 31, and coal on most levels. There's been a lot of research into what ore is found in what concentrations at what levels. Long story short, for the greatest chances of finding all the rarer ores, as well as common ores, dig down to level 11. To see what level you are at, open up your Debug screen by pressing F3. In your x, y, and z coordinates, the y coordinate will show you what level you are at. (It will actually show you what level your feet are at, and what approximate level your eyes are at!)

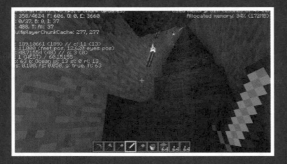

On average, you'll find the most ores of all types at level 11. To check your level, open your debug screen and look at the Y coordinate.

Another way to get to bedrock is to just dig down to bedrock and count up the blocks from there. Now, some people swear by mining at level 10, and others by level 12. So you are probably doing fine at any of these levels.

Efficient Exits

Conserve energy on your mining returns. Instead of jumping up all the steps on the way back, place stair blocks on the steps.

Jumping up mine steps can sap your energy, so consider placing stairs on top of those blocks. You can travel stairs with no extra energy loss.

Or, instead of digging steps down, create a ladder shaft. (Remember not to dig straight down for a ladder shaft. Dig two blocks wide down, moving from block 1 to block 2 as you dig the next block down, placing the ladder pieces along one side.)

To dig a ladder shaft straight down, dig one block in front of you, hop into that, and dig the block you were just standing on. Repeat, placing ladder pieces along one side.

Space-Efficient Entries

If you don't want to travel far from your starting point at ground level, or you just want to use space more efficiently, create a spiral staircase. The tightest spiral staircase takes up a 2×2 block area. To make it, dig one block in front of you. Step into that hole, turn right, and dig the block in front of you and one block down. Step into that hole, turn right, and dig out the next step. Keep doing that until you get down as far as you want to go. You can make wider spiral staircases, too!

Spiral staircases and ladder shafts save space so you aren't traveling too far in one direction from where you start the descent.

Branch Mining

When you really just want to get as much stuff as possible, one of the most efficient ways to get the most ore out of a big area is through branch mining. You start off with a central room or hall and then mine corridors off from that, spacing the corridors four blocks apart (with three blocks between each corridor). If you want to make sure you see every single possible piece of ore, keep two blocks between the corridors. But since most veins of ores are a couple blocks long or more, you can save time and not lose much by placing your shafts four blocks apart.

A branch mine has shafts dug out every three or four blocks.

Cave Mining

If you're fine with battling mobs as you go, or you mine in Peaceful mode, use your world's caves and ravines as your mines. With cave mining, also called spelunking, there's a lot less digging, so it's fast! Follow the cave branches to the lowest they go, then dig with a pickaxe deeper down to level 11 and start a branch mine from there. One way to minimize the mobs is to fully explore and light it with torches first.

TNT

You can find blocks of TNT in desert temples (in traps!), or you can create it from sand (red or yellow) and gunpowder. A TNT blast will create a hole in a mountain or the ground. While it will blow out some whole blocks, most blocks are destroyed. It's not a great tactic for collecting ore, but it is a fun option for making a crater! Place your TNT, "prime it" (meaning light it) by right-clicking with your flint and steel, and step away fast. TNT blocks flash several times before they detonate, giving you time to escape. If you don't mind losing ore on your way down, you can blast your way down to lower levels.

If for some reason you need to blow a big hole in something, use TNT. While a TNT blast does scatter some blocks, it destroys most of them, so it isn't a great option for getting ore.

Build a Base

Once you've reached level 11, or wherever you want to start mining from, make a base camp. If you are planning to spend some time down there, you'll want a protected area with a bed and a chest or two to store your findings. Also place a furnace or two so you can smelt your ores as you mine, as well as a crafting table to make more shovels and pickaxes.

Build a base camp when you are down in your mine.

Enchanted Mining

Enchant your diamond pickaxe, axe, and shovel! The Efficiency enchantment increases your mining speed. Silk Touch lets you collect some blocks that you can't get otherwise, like emerald ore (which you'd normally collect as a single emerald, rather than a block). Unbreaking makes your tools more durable, and Fortune gives you a chance of collecting more ore per block.

Obsidian

Obsidian is the toughest block in Minecraft except for bedrock (which you can't mine) and is a great building material against creepers. It is also required for building Nether portals and enchantment tables. Although it is pretty rare, you can find it in low levels, often by lava. Obsidian is created when running water hits a lava source, and there is plenty of lava at low levels when you mine. You can re-create this yourself, or be very careful when mining it, as there is a good chance that lava is nearby, even under one layer of obsidian. If you see the source of flowing water, there is a chance that digging will release the flow, pushing you around. One tactic is to block the flowing water so you have no surprises when you are digging out the obsidian.

Obsidian, the toughest block except for bedrock, is formed when lava meets running water.

More Tips on Mining

- Have blocks of stone or dirt at the ready in case you need to block a lava or water flow.

- To get rid of a column of gravel at once, destroy the bottom block and quickly place a torch in its place. The torch will destroy the gravel blocks falling down from above.

- Place torches no more than twelve blocks apart to keep the light level high enough to prevent mobs spawning. Use more torches if there are corners in the walls blocking light.

- To gather all the rails in an abandoned mineshaft, just pour a bucket of water into one end—the flowing water will pull up all the rails, ready to pop into your inventory.

CHAPTER 5

FIGHTING

Unless you've been playing in Creative mode or at Peaceful difficulty, you have been attacked by zombies, spiders, and skeletons and have lived to see the day. Now you want to improve your skills and up your chances of coming out on the winning side. If you want to make it through the Nether to gather rare items and travel to the End to defeat the dragon, you'll need to hone your tactics.

Practice, Practice, Practice!

One way to improve your skills is to create a world that's only for practicing fighting. Don't worry about how many times you are killed. Create the world with cheats turned on and start in Creative mode. Use your creative mode inventory to place chests of armor, weapons, chests, food, and everything else you need, then switch back to Survival. Set your difficulty level at whatever you are comfortable with and wait for the mobs with your sword ready. If you are experienced with downloading maps or have some help with this, you can also download maps that have been created by other users, just for practicing. (See Chapter 16: The End and Beyond on page 138 to find out more about maps.) They may have contraptions that spawn zombies or a target practice range. You can also easily create your own valley and build targets to shoot. For moving targets, populate your shooting range with sheep using Creative mode sheep spawners. Add a mountain ledge to shoot from and a chest or more of arrows, and practice your bow and arrow skills!

If you need bow and arrow practice, make your own shooting range! Create a target from dyed wool and fill the range with passive mobs to shoot at.

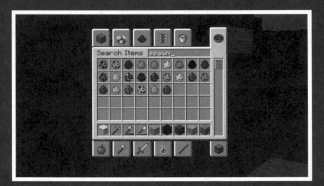

In Creative mode, your inventory includes spawn eggs for each type of mob. Place an egg on the ground to spawn the mob.

Attack!

Whenever possible, attack, and attack fast. Attacking fast means the mob has less time to get you and fewer opportunities to strike you. Use continuous clicking of your sword for spiders, zombies, slime, and creepers. When you can, use your sword to block blows and arrows by right-clicking.

If you're too close to a skeleton, right-click to block its arrows.

This can decrease the damage done to you by up to 50 percent. (When you block, you move at a slow speed.) Practice flailing or block-hitting. Quickly alternate between attack (left-click) and block (right-click). If you are too close to an exploding creeper, use a block to try to reduce the damage. When you deliver damage to a mob, it turns red. While it is red, you can't deliver any more damage, so wait a moment or fight a different mob. If you can, lead them to a better fighting area. Most mobs switch to a pursuit mode if they are within sixteen blocks of you and can directly see you. Once they are in pursuit they don't stop, so you can lead them directly to a cleverly placed lava pool or cliff.

Critical Hits

To make the most of your attack, jump and deliver your blow as you fall. This gives a critical hit that delivers up to 50 percent more damage, and this can make a huge difference. You can tell you've delivered a critical hit when stars float over your opponent. You can also deliver a critical hit when jumping off a block. A critical hit with an arrow occurs if your arrow is fully pulled back before you shoot. You can tell your arrow is fully charged when your bow shakes slightly.

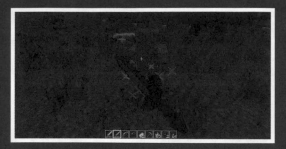

To cause the most damage, jump and then swing on your way down for a critical hit. If you give one, you'll see little stars over your victim.

Knockbacks

If you are sprinting before the blow, you knock back the enemy. Knocking back a creeper may give you more time to escape. However, knocking back a skeleton gives it a chance to re-arm, so don't use this tactic with them. You can knock back entities with chicken eggs or snowballs.

Minecraft Enemies

Cave Spiders

Cave spiders only spawn from a spawner, a box found in dungeons and mineshafts. They are faster than regular spiders and poisonous. If you come across a spawner, get rid of any cobwebs, as these will slow you down and not the spider. Break the spawner with a pickaxe. If you want to save the spawner for later use in a mob farm, disable it. Put torches around all sides and the top to keep the light level high, or surround it with cobblestone.

A cave spider spawner in a dungeon. Disarm a spawner by placing torches around and on top. You can destroy the spawner with your pickaxe.

Creepers

If a creeper is suddenly next to you, run away. You have about 1.5 seconds, once it starts detonating, to get about five blocks away. If you do, the creeper will halt the process. It will still be after you, though! Try to get far away from them and then attack them with a bow. If you need to fight them close up, hit them and then back away quickly or try to knock the creeper back.

Enderman

Pour water at its feet to damage it without provoking it. Making sure your crosshairs don't move above its legs (so as not to provoke it), attack its feet.

Endermites

Endermites are small like silverfish. They are weak (8 hearts) so just slash at them quickly.

Guardians and Elder Guardians

You'll need a sharp sword and potions. Corner them quickly inside the monument so they can't escape.

Silverfish

These small, bug-like mobs hide in silverfish blocks that look like stone or granite in Extreme Hill biomes and in stronghold dungeons. If you break one of these blocks, the silverfish, and sometimes surrounding silverfish, will come out to attack you as a group. To kill them, use a steel and flint to set them on fire, or drop a bucket of lava on them (stand on a block to do this!). You can also drop gravel on them. If you attack them indirectly like this without a sword, it stops them from alerting their allies.

Skeletons

Use your A and D keys to sidestep their arrows, or circle them as you attack. Skeletons will try to circle around you to attack you from behind, so watch out behind you.

Slime

Attack them from above. Kill the big ones first, then move to the smaller ones.

Spiders

Because of their jumping abilities, hit them and walk backward.

Spider Jockeys
Kill the skeleton first and then the spider.

Witches
Because they can throw potions at you, kill witches with a bow. Or move very fast to attack the witch before it has time to drink Fire Resistant and Instant Health potions to protect itself.

Use your bow to kill witches, or attack them before they drink their potion and splash you with one.

Zombies
Hitting a zombie can draw others to the fight, so first see if you can lead them outside to burn in the sun.

Zombie XP farm
Mob experience farms are ways to get lots of experience points (XP). These farms create large numbers of mobs in an enclosed space as well as a safe place for you to kill them. In a simple zombie XP farm, first find a zombie mob spawner in a dungeon and disarm it. Build a 8 x 8 chamber around the spawner, with a 2×1 shaft along one of the longest walls, in the center. The shaft should be less than twenty-three blocks deep. (A twenty-two-block fall will leave creepers, zombies, and skeletons with a

half heart of life left, so they'll be fast to kill and provide experience orbs.) You can use water flows to push the zombies to the
pit. When you pour water, the water flows for eight blocks and
then stops. Use a bucket to pour water at the opposite corners
from the shaft. The two water flows should stop at the edge of
the shaft, without going into the shaft. (If they don't, you may
need to make the room a block or two bigger.)

Enclose the zombie spawner so that water placed at one side will
push zombies through a shaft at the other end.

Next, on the outside of the chamber, and on the outside of the
zombie shaft, create another ladder shaft for you that is one
block deeper. Dig a 1×1 hole between you and the zombie shaft
so you can attack the zombies' feet with a sword. You will need
to plan your build so that you can re-arm the spawner, barricade
the room, then get down your ladder shaft to your killing cubi-
cle! There are hundreds of types of mob spawners and tutorials
online with different ways to kill mobs of mobs. For a different
type of mob farming that gets you more loot without moving a
muscle, see the mob farm instructions in chapter 8.

Build your separate access to the zombie drop so that there is a one-block-high hole you can attack them through.

More Mob Fighting Tips

- For extra defense, tame wolves and ocelots. Tamed wolves will attack your enemies in battle and a tamed ocelot will scare creepers away.

- A creeper that is hit with lightning becomes "charged" with a bluish light and then can deliver even more explosive force—more than a TNT block.

- Running from a creeper? By sprinting and jumping at the same time, you'll go faster than if you are just sprinting.

- You can wear a pumpkin on your head and look at an Enderman without provoking it.

- Endermen need a forty-two-block drop to leave them with half a heart. Spiders need an eighteen-block drop.

CHAPTER 6

ANIMALS

Animals are essential to surviving and thriving in your Minecraft world. You use them to help and protect you, give you food, and keep you company! Animals are a type of mob in Minecraft called a passive mob, because they don't attack you. By now you've probably tamed and bred sheep, chicken, goats, and pigs, but there is much more fun to have with them.

Where do you find the animals? Sheep, horses, and cows like open fields with grass. Go to a jungle to find an ocelot, and go to forests and plains for pigs. To lure animals back to your farm, use the same items as you would to breed them. With the lured item in your hand, get close to the animal. When you see the animal turn to look at you and take a few steps toward you, it is interested! Make your way slowly back home with the lure item in your hand. Sometimes animals lose interest, so keep an eye out for animals that have stopped following you. You will need to re-interest them!

Mooshroom

A mooshroom is one of the strangest and rarest animals! It looks like a cow painted as a red mushroom, with red mushrooms growing on its back. The only place you can find them is on a rare Mushroom Island biome. You can milk a mooshroom with an empty bowl for mushroom stew! And if you shear the mushrooms off its back, it will turn back into a cow.

The mooshroom is a hybrid cow/mushroom. If you shave its mushrooms, it turns back into a cow.

The mushroom biome also grows giant mushrooms on a special dirt-like block called mycelium. You can break a giant mushroom for a mushroom harvest.

The Mushroom Island biome is rare, and it's the only place you can find the mooshroom creature!

Wolf Pets

Unlike farm animals and ocelots, wolves are actually a neutral mob, like Endermen. If you attack a wolf, you will be attacked back, likely by its whole pack. Once you tame a wolf, though, it is a protective friend. It will follow you wherever you go and attack anything that attacks you. If your wolf is far from you and you are attacked, it will teleport to you. Unlike farm animals, wolves need to be fed. You can tell how healthy a wolf is by its tail. If it's sticking straight out, it's doing great. Its tail starts to angle down as it loses health, but a meal of meat (cooked is best) will help restore it. Tamed and wild wolves attack skeletons automatically, and skeletons will run from them!

You can tell a wolf is healthy if its tail is straight out. If your wolf's tail droops, it is time to feed it.

Tame an Ocelot

Creepers are scared of ocelots! Tame an ocelot so it will help stop creepers getting close to your home. An ocelot can only be tamed if it is in begging mode, which means it is slowly walking toward you and looking at you. But you can't make any sudden moves or turns or it will stop begging and go away. Taming an ocelot is a tricky business. One tactic you might want to consider is leashing it first, then continuing to tempt it with fish.

Keep very still as you try to tame an ocelot. It may flee with sudden movements.

Taming and Riding Horses

Riding a horse is the fastest way to travel in Survival mode. They can jump up to four blocks high, ride over one-block holes in the ground, and jump over larger holes. To keep a horse, you will need to find a wild one, tame it, and outfit it with a saddle. To tame a horse, you must mount it by right-clicking on it with your hand. The horse will probably throw you off, so keep doing this until hearts float above its head and it lets you stay on. It may take five or more tries.

To dismount the horse, use the sneak key. Now the horse is tamed, but it won't follow you around like a tamed wolf or ocelot. You will need to either ride it or keep a lead on it and tie the lead to a fence post. You craft a lead with string and slimeball.

In order to ride the horse, place a saddle on it by right-clicking on the saddle. (To get a rare Minecraft saddle, you will have to trade with a villager or find one in a chest.) If you are on the horse already, open your inventory. Your inventory contains a horse inventory slot now, and you can place the saddle into these slots. You can also outfit your horse with armor. Like saddles, horse armor can only be found in chests.

The horse inventory appears above your horse. To saddle a horse, drag a saddle to it.

You can ride a horse in the same way you move about, with the keyboard controls and mouse. You will also see, above your hotbar, the horse's jump bar in place of your experience bar. Your health bar is replaced with the horse's health bar.

When you ride a horse, your display shows the horse's health and a jump bar in place of your health and experience bars.

More Horse Tips

- To make your horse jump, hold down the jump key (space bar) and release when you are ready. Some horses can jump up four or more blocks high.

- You can fight on horses, just like on foot, as well as mine and collect dropped items.

- Breed horses with golden apples or golden carrots. Golden apples are rare items you can find sometimes in dungeon chests. You craft a golden carrot from eight golden nuggets and a regular carrot.

- Feed foals (young horses) so they grow faster. To restore the health of damaged horses, feed them with wheat, sugar, apples, bread, hay bales, and golden carrots and apples. Hay bales are made from nine blocks of wheat. (If you place a hay bale into your crafting table, it will give nine blocks of wheat. This makes it a great way to travel with lots of wheat!)

- Not all horses are the same—some are faster and can jump higher than others.

- Horses don't like water, and you will be dismounted if you ride in water deeper than two blocks. You may need to use a lead to get them through water. With a leashed horse, you can even get in a boat and travel over an ocean.

- You can also leash wild horses.

Donkeys

Donkeys are smaller than horses, have a grayish-brown coat, and have tall ears. Like horses, though, they can be fed and bred the same way. You can place a chest on them and fill the chest up with supplies! You create mules only by breeding a horse with a donkey. Mules look like donkeys but have a darker coat. They can also be equipped with a chest.

Right-click a tamed donkey or mule with a chest. The donkey's inventory will hold fifteen items.

Fun with Pigs

You can ride a pig! Make a carrot on a stick (a carrot and a new fishing pole), place a saddle on your pig, and jump on! Direct the pig with the carrot. Eventually, the pig will eat the carrot, and you will no longer be able to control your pig. In Creative mode, you can fly a pig! In Creative mode, leash any animal and it will fly when you do! You have to be very gentle coming down to the ground, though. What about flying a pig—off a cliff? There is actually an achievement called When Pigs Fly. You will need to ride a pig to the edge of a cliff and get him to jump off, for example, by hitting it. But watch out: you both may die. One other trick with a pig is to push it into a minecraft, saddle it, and hop on. This will power the minecraft!

To ride a pig, place a saddle on it. Control it with a carrot on a stick (actually a fishing rod).

Animal Farms

When you design your animal enclosures, be sure to add in a double gate system. This adds an additional exterior pen as a fenced and gated walkway. That way, when an animal escapes its pen (and they all do at some point), it will still be fenced in within the general enclosure, and you will have a much easier time getting them back in their pen. If you are breeding chickens, remember they can jump over a single-block high fence, so you'll need to make their fences higher or dig a level down in their pen.

For animal pens, use a double gated system. If an animal escapes from its pen, there is a second gated pen to prevent it running away.

More Animal Tips

- Squids can't be bred, but you can kill them for sacs of black ink, which you can use as a dye.

- Bats seem to be pretty useless—they don't drop anything or provide food. But they do make a squeaking noise, and if you are digging a mine, hearing that squeak means a cave is nearby.

- Don't kill all the animals in a group. Friendly mobs spawn extremely rarely so you will have lost a potential source of animals. At the very least, leave a couple to breed, or bring two back for your own breeding farm.

- If you kill a sheep, it drops wool (and meat). But you'll get more wool if you use your shears, and the sheep's wool will regrow.

- You can throw a chicken's egg, and sometimes they'll hatch into a chicken on the spot! There's even a rare chance for quadruplets.

- Breed rabbits for their great drops: rabbit meat (for stew), feet (for potions of leaping), and rabbit hide (4 of these will make 1 regular leather.) You can breed rabbits with dandelions and golden carrots as well as carrots.

- If you name a rabbit Toast with a nametag, the rabbit will take on a custom black and white rabbit skin. The skin is a memorial for a pet rabbit that belonged to a friend of one of the game developers.

- You can speed up how fast baby animals turn into adults by feeding them their favorite food (the same used for breeding). Each time you feed it, you will take off about 10 percent of the growth time left.

CHAPTER 7

VILLAGES AND VILLAGERS

ike pyramids and abandoned mineshafts, villages and villagers are a great source for rare items in Minecraft. You can trade for items with villagers, find carrots and potatoes in their farms and books in their libraries, and loot the occasional chest! Villages can be found in the desert, plains, and savanna biomes, although they are pretty rare and not easy to find. Villages in the plains and savanna are built mostly with wood and cobblestone, while villages in the desert are made from sandstone.

A village in the desert and savanna will have the same types of buildings, just constructed with "local" materials.

In addition to huts, houses, and farms, villages have several specialized buildings. You can find butcher shops, libraries, smithies, and churches. Butcher shops have tables and stone slab counters, libraries have bookshelves, smithies have furnaces and a chest, and churches have an altar.

A butcher shop, library, smithy, and church.

Help the Village!

Villages have a hard time surviving because they attract zombies who turn the inhabitants into zombie villagers. If you are playing in Hard difficulty or Hardcore mode, zombies can even break down their wooden doors. You won't be able to trade with a zombie villager, but you will be killed by one. Villagers don't breed quickly, and they can accidentally die by stepping into lava or falling into their wells. Overall, that means a village can have trouble keeping its numbers up.

To cure a zombie villager, isolate it, splash it with a Potion of Weakness, and feed it a golden apple. The villager will shake for a few minutes before it recovers.

How to Help Save a Village

- Sleep inside it as soon as dusk falls. When you sleep, the game changes the time of day to dawn. This means that night is "skipped," along with the darkness that allows mobs to spawn. This minimizes zombies from spawning. In the morning, kill off the zombies.

- Fence the village in. You can also lock villagers in their homes until the fencing is done, to keep them safe.

- Remove stairs in front of doors, replace broken doors, and make sure doors are hung properly from the outside. (Do not add a door to the smithy, though. Because of the way the building is constructed, this confuses the villagers and prompts them to gather outside.)

- Light the outside of the village up to prevent mob spawning.

- Fix hazards, such as nearby cactus, pools of lava, and mob-spawning caves.

- If you can, cure zombie villagers by splashing them with a Potion of Weakness and feeding them a golden apple. It takes a few minutes for a zombie villager to heal, so try to make sure the zombie villager is isolated (and protected from sunlight) and can't hurt other villagers or you in the meantime.

- You can also protect your villagers with Iron Golems, and you can make new houses to increase your village and give them a better chance of survival.

Iron Golems

Iron Golems only spawn naturally if a village has ten villagers and twenty-one houses. If the village doesn't have an Iron Golem, make one. You can create an Iron Golem with a pumpkin or Jack o'Lantern head and four blocks of iron in a T, placed on the ground (not in a crafting table). Iron Golems protect villagers only, and if they aren't in a village, they can wander away. You can keep Iron Golems in a fenced area or leash it to follow you.

Place the pumpkin or lantern last when you make an Iron Golem.

Trading

The types of trading offers that a villager makes to you depend on their job. In general, you buy with emeralds or sell goods to receive emeralds. The first time you trade with a villager, there will be just one offer. They will make new offers once you've traded for the last item in their list and closed the inventory window. If they have a new offer for you, you'll see green and purple particles over their head.

When a villager has a new offer, you will see green and purple particles over him.

There are hundreds of trading offers. Also, different villagers of the same type can offer better or worse deals. One weapon smith might offer a great deal of 12 emeralds for a diamond pick, and another weapon smith's offer might be more expensive. A great tactic is to find several villagers that have good deals giving you emeralds for something you can get easily and for free, and keep them safe and separated so you can find them again. For example, you may find a farmer that will give you 1 emerald for 7 melons. Or a librarian who will give you an emerald for 21 paper. You can then trade with villagers librarians to get masses of emeralds. When the villager's trade expires, you will need to buy something else for a while to get them to re-offer the deal you want. Once you have your emeralds in hand, you then want to find several villagers with the best deals on stuff that is difficult to get in the game. A cleric may have a good deal on Bottles o' Enchanting (3 emeralds is great!), and a tool smith may have a great deal on diamond picks. Here are the villager types and what they trade in:

Armorer: Buys coal, iron, and diamonds; sells axes and swords.
Butcher: Buys raw pork, raw chicken, and coal; sells cooked pork and chicken.
Cleric: Buys zombie flesh and gold; sells lapis, redstone, glowstone, Eyes of Ender, Bottles o' Enchanting, and redstone.
Farmer: Buys farm produce; sells bread, pastries, and apples.
Fisherman: Buys fish, coal, and string; sells fishing rods.
Fletcher: Buys string and gravel; sells bows and arrows.
Leatherworker: Buys leather; sells leather armor and saddles.
Librarian: Buys paper and books; sells enchanted books, compasses, bookshelves, glass, and nametags.
Shepherd: Buys wool; sells wool and shears.
Tool Smith: Buys coal, iron, and diamonds; sells shovels and picks.
Weapon Smith: Buys coal, iron, and diamonds; sells axes and swords.

Eleven types of villagers have five costumes. A cleric is in purple, and armorers, tool smiths, and weapon smiths are in black. Librarians wear white, and butchers and leatherworkers have a white apron. Farmers, fishermen, fletchers, and shepherds all wear brown.

Increase the Population

Add new houses to the village. In order for the Minecraft program to recognize you have made a new house, it must first see a new door. To make sure that the door counts as a house, the program checks to see if there is a roof on one side of the door. As long as you follow these guidelines, you can make your village houses however you like. Because of the way the program works, you can build a door with just one block of roof. Here is what the program looks for: After you've built a door, it looks at the five spaces directly in front of and in back of the door to check for roof blocks. A roof block is any block preventing sunlight from hitting the ground. There must be more roof blocks on one side of the door than the other. (This means you can make a house from just a block of dirt and a door, if you are low on resources.) Finally, to count as a house, the door must be near a villager. For every three-and-a-half new doors, a new villager will be created, so to get two villagers, make seven doors. For the villagers to make children, there must be at least two villagers.

To add the simplest village house, you just need a door and one roof block behind it.

Be Nice!

You have a popularity score with each village. It starts at 0, increases to a high of 10, and can decrease to -30. Trading with a villager for the last offer slot in their inventory adds one point. You get points taken off for attacking a villager (-1), killing a villager (-2), killing a village child (-3), and killing the village's Iron Golem (-5). If you have a score of -15, the village's Iron Golem will attack you.

More Village Tips

- Zombie sieges happen more often in large villages with forty or more villagers.

- Villages spawn more frequently in the superflat terrain and in worlds created with the Large Biomes option.

- Village wells are an easy place for players and villagers to fall in, and they are too deep to jump out of. Put blocks at the bottom of the well so they aren't a death trap.

Putting blocks at the bottom of a well will prevent villagers from drowning.

CHAPTER 8

BUILDING

Your home in Minecraft can be anything from a temporary shelter while you explore the world or a massive fortress that keeps you safe from the mobs. There's no right way to build your home—it all depends on how you play your game and what you want.

There are many great places to build a home, too. Build on a cliff or mountain, or build a tower if you want a great lookout. If you build on flat land, you'll have an easier time expanding with farms and contraptions. If you need shelter in a hurry, mine into the side of a mountain. You can even set your home up in a cave, walling off areas as you need. You can build a treehouse, or even build your home under water. If you don't want to build too much but want a pretty nice home, think about taking over a village home or even a temple. (For a village home, be prepared to battle and defend against extra zombies looking for villager snacks.)

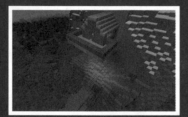

You have endless choices for building your Minecraft base. Make the swamps your home, or disguise your home as a tree!

In any location you choose, there are ways to make sure the home you build is safe from creeper explosions and unexpected spider attacks. One thing to keep in mind is whether your defensive building techniques are putting you in danger in addition to the mobs. You don't want to fall into your own cactus and lava pits! Possibly the safest home is one built underground and well lit, where no mobs can spawn.

A fairly simple way to protect your homestead is to guard it with a full perimeter wall three blocks high. The wall should have an overhang (using slabs) to prevent spiders from jumping over it, or a top layer of glass (which spiders can't climb), and should also be well lit. Make sure the area outside your defending wall is clear, and that there are no trees or high ground that a mob can jump on to get over the wall.

A three-block-high defensive perimeter wall with a lip to stop spiders from crawling over.

For extra flair, make a way to help kill stray mobs coming up to your house. On the outside of the wall, dig a series of two-block-deep pits for mobs to fall into. On the inside of the wall, dig yourself a tunnel or a short ladder shaft to access your pits. You should be one level deeper than the mob pit. Make a one block hole between your side and the foot of the pit. This is often called a "murder hole." It allows you to attack the feet of the trapped mobs and gather the loot they drop.

Two-block-deep pits outside your defensive wall to trap mobs. On the inside of the wall, make a murder hole from where you can kill them.

More Tips on Defensive Building

- Spiders can't climb up glass or iron bars, and an overhang on a wall will stop them from climbing over.

- The strongest block is obsidian—it won't be damaged by creeper explosions. If you don't have lots of rare obsidian to spare, build cobblestone walls that are five blocks high and three or four blocks deep. If you are short on cobblestone, make a cobblestone wall one block thick and use dirt or wood on the inside and outside. If you have no cobblestone, just use dirt or wood.

- Light up your roof to stop mobs spawning there. In fact, light up all your outside areas to minimize spawning.

- Because zombies can break through wood doors in Hard difficulty or Hardcore mode, use iron doors with buttons.

- Except for spiders, mobs can't cross a ditch that is one block wide and two blocks deep.

- Pour water into a ditch so that it flows to a trap or to an exit point. This way, mobs will flow from wherever they fall into the trap.

- Snow Golems will knock back mobs with their snow-balls, and give some small damage to blazes and the Ender Dragon. Their snowballs will also cause Ender-men to teleport. You can build a defensive barricade around your home filled with Snow Golems. It should be roofed so they aren't damaged by rain and fenced in so they don't wander. (Also, Snow Golems will melt in warmer biomes, like deserts.) You could also cre-ate mini guard towers for single Snow Golems, one or two blocks off the ground. To create a Snow Go-lem, place two snow blocks (made from four snow-balls each) on top of each other on the ground and top with a pumpkin. Because Snow Golems attract hostile mobs, you can use them to lure mobs into a trap, such as a lava pit. Snow Golems can be killed by skeletons, and they don't attack creepers.

- In addition to tamed wolves, keep pet cats, to frighten creepers, and a pet Iron Golem, to attack any mobs.

- Because Endermen can teleport anywhere, build nooks inside and out that are only two blocks high (or two-and-a-half blocks high, by using slabs) that you can retreat to and fight them from.

How Big?

Your house doesn't need to be huge. Most important is that it provides a safe place to sleep and use your stuff. So to start with, it needs to be big enough for your bed, your crafting table, a fur-nace, and a chest. As you progress, you'll want to have space for an enchanting table and bookshelves and a brewing station, as well as more furnaces and a lot more chests. If you are brewing a lot, you'll want a 2×2 well to get water from.

Probably the most important of all are your chests. If you mine, farm, and build a lot, you will end up needing many to store all your goods. One way to organize chests so that you can easily find everything quickly is keep all items of one type or category in separate chests. For example, all rare ore and metals in one chest, all building materials (cobblestone, fences) in another chest, and all plant material in another chest. You can place doubled-up chests above each other on a wall and place signs to say what's in them. (You can add four lines of text to a sign. To move up and down lines, use your up and down arrow keys.)

Make room for plenty of chests in your home, and make signs so you know what is where.

Expanding

In addition to your shelter, as you expand you might want to add other types of structures to your home base—a map room to display your maps, a dock for your boats and for fishing, farms, and a watchtower or lookout. For extra protection, you can surround your home base with a massive stone wall. A helpful build near your home is a mob farm—one that just gathers and kills mobs for you, so you just need to retrieve their drops. Because mobs spawn at least twenty-four blocks away from you, you need to build your mob farm twenty-four blocks away from where you usually are—or twenty-four blocks or more in the air!

Emergency Shelters

Sometimes you need a nighttime shelter, and fast. You know how to dig into a mountain and close it up for a quick shelter. You can also dig three blocks down and place dirt blocks above you. Or pillar jump with dirt or gravel blocks fifteen blocks up (to stay out of the range of skeleton arrows) and stay up there. If you carry a bed, dig out enough space or make a platform big enough for it so you can sleep through the night.

Build a Simple Mob Farm

Mob farms are popular builds in Minecraft. Some mob farms are built to gather experience, like the zombie spawner farm explained in chapter 5. These gather mobs in one place so you can kill them and get the experience orbs. Other mob farms are built to automatically kill mobs and gather the loot they drop without giving you any experience—these contraptions are also called mob grinders. How fast a mob farm spawns and kills mobs depends on game mechanic factors like the conditions a mob will spawn in. For example, Endermen can only spawn in spaces that are three blocks high. Players have built hundreds of designs for mob farms and grinders. One of the simplest mob killing farms you can build is a closed-in, cobblestone room built twenty-eight blocks above the ground. (It is safest, and easiest, if you build this in Creative mode.) The reason to have this so high is that mobs spawn at least twenty-four blocks away from you. This farm also uses a long drop from the top to kill the mobs.[1]

(a) Build a 20×20 square floor, twenty-eight blocks up from ground level. This will be the base of the spawning chamber.

(b) Make a two-block-wide and two-block-deep trench from the center of one side to the opposite side, starting one block in from the outer edge. Dig an identical trench across the other side.

Partway done. The trenches that cross your spawning chamber should be two blocks deep and two blocks wide.

(c) In the middle of the crossing trenches, dig a 2×2 hole. (You can line the trenches with signs if you have them. Signs make mobs think that there is a block in the space. They trick the mob into walking into empty space where they will drop.)

(d) Now, at each of the four outer ends of the trenches, pour water against both corners of the outside wall blocks to make water flow along the trench towards the center. Because the trenches are eight blocks long, the water stops at the edge of the hole. This is where mobs will be pushed and drop. The drop to the ground (where you will place hoppers and chests to collect the drops) will kill them.

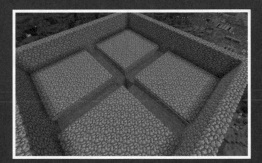

The spawning chamber is ready to be closed in.

(e) Build walls three blocks high around the base. Fill these in with a roof so you are leaving only two blocks of empty space in the spawning chamber.

(f) To know where to place the bottom collection point, build a 2×2 wall from one of the edges of the 2×2 hole down to the ground.

(g) Place two chests at the bottom of the wall and two hoppers above these, using Shift and right-clicking. In front of the two hoppers, place another two hoppers. The four hoppers need to be exactly underneath the 2×2 hole in the spawning chamber. Place four slabs on top of the hoppers, by pressing Shift and right-clicking.

On the ground directly beneath the spawning chamber's 4×4 hole, place two chests with four hoppers above.

(h) Now build out the chimney back up to the hole in the farm above. So you can see the mobs dropping and dying, use glass blocks at the bottom of the chimney.

The finished mob farm with the enclosed shaft. You can use glass at the bottom of the shaft to see your doomed mobs splat. Once the mobs start dropping, right-click on your chests to collect your loot.

Mob farms can be incredibly complex, and you can find many examples and tutorials online and on YouTube. Another popular structure to build is an automatic farm. These use pistons, redstone, and often water to automatically harvest your crop.

CHAPTER 9

FARMING

arming is the best way in Minecraft to make sure you have a steady supply of food coming in. A farm also means you don't waste too much time hunting and gathering, so you can have more time for mining, exploring, and building. And it's fun, too! Once your seeds are planted and growing, the harvested food will provide enough seeds or starter crop for you to grow the next crop. While wheat is the most important crop, because it can make bread, try out all the different seeds. You can farm carrots, potatoes, melons, pumpkins, and cocoa beans in pretty much the same way as wheat. It takes two to three days for a crop to fully grow. Once the crop is mature, you can leave it there until you are ready to collect it. When you are planning your farm, choose an area that is as flat as possible, and use your shovel to even the ground out. Make a shed to keep a crafting table and chest for farming supplies, like hoes and seeds, close by.

Where to Find the Seeds

Wheat
Break tall grass to gather wheat seeds. You use wheat to make bread, cookies, and cake, but you can also use it to lure and breed sheep and cows (and mooshrooms!).

Carrots and Potatoes

You can find carrots and potatoes in village farms. Sometimes they are dropped by zombies.

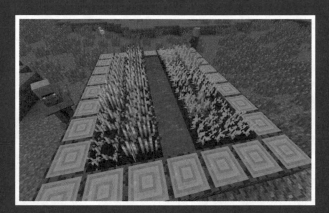

You can find carrots and potatoes in village farms.

Carrots and potatoes don't have seeds, you just plant the item and replant from your harvested crop. Watch out, though— every once in a while, a potato crop will give a poisonous potato. It has green patches on it, is a tiny bit smaller than a regular potato, and will poison you if you eat it. You can't cook it or plant it.

A poisonous potato (left) and a regular one (right).

Melon and Pumpkin Seeds

You can find seeds in the chests of abandoned mineshafts. You can also buy them whole from villagers or find wild melons and pumpkins growing. Melons grow in jungles, while pumpkins grow in many biomes. When you plant them, first a stalk will grow, and then the fruit appears in a block next to the stalk.

You can find pumpkin growing in many biomes, but look for wild melons in the jungle. You can also find seeds in dungeon chests.

You will need to plant these seeds on farmland and make sure there are empty grass, dirt, or farmland blocks next to them. To harvest, gather the fruit only—leave the stem and it will grow more fruit! You can't use bone meal to grow a full pumpkin or melon. Bone meal will grow their stems though. The fastest way to harvest pumpkins and melons is with an axe.

Be careful when you are farming. Jumping on farmland can turn it back into dirt. It is very easy to forget and walk on it. To be safe, make clear pathways of cobblestone between rows of crops to walk on, and fence your farm in to stop mobs from walking on it. Or, you can create a raised bed farm by placing rows of dirt blocks and planting on top.

A raised bed farm will help keep you from trampling the farmland.

To make your crops grow as fast as they can, make sure the farmland is watered and that your crops have light during the night. To water the farmland, there must be a source of water within four blocks. If you don't have a bucket yet to gather water, plant near a pond. One standard tactic is to make a 9 × 9 block of farmland with the center block dug out and filled with water. This leaves each farmland block within four blocks of water. Crops also grow faster if they are planted next to other types of crops. You don't need to make sure that each crop is next to a different crop, just have rows of different crops next to each other.

Use a 9×9 block plot for the most efficient watering.

Crops mature to harvesting within three Minecraft days. You can make this closer to two days if the ground is watered, you plant in rows of different crops, you keep the edge of the farm plot as empty, watered farmland, and you keep the crops lit at night by placing torches on the surrounding fence.

If you have iron, you can make a bucket with three ingots. To get water from a river, lake, or sea, just right-click the bucket on the water. To make a never-ending supply of water, do the following: Dig a 2×2 hole, one block deep. Fill two corners opposite from each other with water. Now you can fill your bucket as many times as you need!

For an endless water supply, pour water into two opposite corners of a 2×2 hole.

Close to Home

Because of the way memory is used in the programming of Minecraft, if you stray too far from home, the growth rate of your crops slows to nothing. So for the fastest growth, keep within a couple hundred blocks of your farm.

When Is It Done?

Wheat is ready to harvest when the tops turn brown, and carrots are ready when you see the orange tops stick out. Potato is mature when you see the brown tops emerge. A melon or pumpkin is ready as soon as the melon or pumpkin block appears on an adjacent block.

As soon as a melon or pumpkin appears next to a stalk, it is ready to pluck.

Sugar Cane Farm

You use sugar cane to make sugar for cake and pumpkin pie. But you also use it to make paper for maps and books, as well as fermented spider eyes and the Potion of Swiftness. Once you are established, it can be a good idea to have your own sugar cane farm so you have a steady supply for paper, maps, and books. You can find sugar cane on your travels growing alongside water.

Sugar cane should be planted with one side next to water.

Since sugar cane doesn't have seeds, you will need to collect the sugar cane blocks and plant these. Sugar cane grows on sand, grass, or dirt, and the block needs to have at least one side next to water. One easy way to grow sugar cane is to plant rows, two blocks wide, into a pond. Leave one block of pond left between each row. This way, each sugar cane farm block is next to water. Sugar cane grows slowly to only three blocks high, even though wild sugar cane can grow higher. To harvest, you can break just the second block of the sugar cane—this will make both the second and third blocks fall, ready to collect. And this leaves the bottom block in place to grow more sugar cane.

Cocoa Bean Farm

Cocoa beans grow in cocoa pods on jungle trees. Breaking a cocoa pod gives you a group of beans. To grow cocoa beans, you place blocks of jungle wood (it does not have to be a growing tree), then place cocoa beans on the side of this. Don't harvest cocoa pods until they mature and are colored orange-brown. Unripe cocoa pods only give one cocoa bean, and mature pods give two or three. You use cocoa to make brown dye, stain clay, glass, and wool brown, and make cookies and brown firework stars.

Grow cocoa beans on any blocks of jungle wood.

CHAPTER 10

FOOD AND FISHING

If you are playing in Survival mode on any difficulty beyond Peaceful, you will need to make sure you never get too hungry, because being too hungry drops your health points. (However, if you are playing on Easy or Normal levels, you won't die from starvation.) Both sprinting and jumping make you hungry. If your hunger goes below 6, you can't sprint. Eating something fills your hunger bar, and it helps rebuild your health, too. Also, when you are less hungry, you gain health more quickly.

Saturation Point

In addition to the hunger bar, you also have a hidden score called "saturation," which depends on the type of food you have eaten. Your hunger bar doesn't go down until your saturation reaches 0. You can tell your saturation level is at 0 when your hunger bar gets shaky, and that's when you'll start losing hunger points. Different activities can reduce your saturation level. Jumping while you sprint causes the biggest drop in saturation. Other actions that make the biggest hit on saturation include being poisoned, fighting, jumping, and sprinting. Different foods give you different saturation points and different hunger points. Cooking meat gives more saturation points. The top foods for hunger points are cake, rabbit stew, pumpkin pie, cooked porkchop, and steak. The top foods for saturation are golden carrot, porkchop, steak, and rabbit stew. Finally, the top four foods with the best overall food and saturation value rabbit stew, porkchop, steak, and golden carrot. The top overall? Rabbit stew, for 10 hunger points and 12 saturation. Make it with rabbit, mushroom, carrot, baked potato, and a bowl.

You can be poisoned from eating pufferfish or spider eyes or by Witches or cave spiders. Poison won't kill you but can drop you to half a heart. It will also make your screen blur and wave and your health and hunger bars go greenish.

When Poison Is Good

In an emergency, you can eat raw chicken, rotten meat, and even spider eyes. They will give you poisoning, but you will recover if you are healthy. If you have milk from a cow to drink, you will recover faster. Eating a spider eye costs four damage points, but if you are desperate and need some hunger points to start healing, it can be a good solution.

Cook and Kill

You can cook your meat as you kill it, by lighting the ground an animal is on with flint and steel before you kill it. The animal will drop cooked meat instead of raw.

Firing up a cow before killing it will get you a cooked steak instead of raw.

More Food Tips

- You can't eat cake unless it's been placed on a block.

- Eating several raw chickens will give you more hunger points than the poisoning can take away.

- If you eat while moving, you slow down. However, you can eat on a ladder without slowing down.

- To milk a cow, hold a bucket and right-click the cow.

- Mooshrooms supply mushroom stew instead of milk. If you have a mooshroom, you have an endless supply of stew. To milk (or mushroom stew) a mooshroom, hold a bowl and right-click it.

Milk a cow by right-clicking it with an empty bucket and a mooshroom by right-clicking it with a wooden bowl.

- If you know you'll be fighting, eat the foods with the greatest value: rabbit stew, porkchop, steak, and golden carrot. Take them into combat with you, too, to eat when recovering from damage.

Fishing for Food

Rainy day? You can sleep in your bed during a thunderstorm, even if it isn't night! Or better yet, fish—there are more fish during rain than when it's clear. Ordinarily, fishing outside will get you a fish in less than forty-five seconds. If it's raining, your chances improve by about 20 percent.

Craft a fishing rod from sticks and string, and right-click on water while holding the rod to cast the line. Watch the bobber. When a fish is ready to bite, you will see a small trail of bubbles. When the bobber dips below the water, right-click to bring the line and fish in. The fish will fly at you, sometimes over your head, before it drops to the ground. Often it will fly straight into your inventory.

Right before a fish bites, you'll see a trail of bubbles. When the bobber dips, the fish is caught, so quickly right-click to bring in the catch.

Sometimes you can catch treasure or junk with the fishing rod. Fishing treasure can be saddles, lily pads, name tags, enchanted but used bows and fishing rods, and enchanted books. Fishing can also bring you junk—stuff like bowls, leather, squid ink sacs, leather boots, sticks, string, damaged bows and fishing rods, trip wire hooks, water bottles, and bones. So sometimes you might want junk! With an enchanted rod, you have a greater chance of catching treasure instead of junk.

Beyond Fishing

You can use your fishing rod to hook other entities, like mobs. Drag a zombie into lava! Drag a skeleton over a cliff! Hooking a mob with a fishing rod counts as an attack and will drop the durability of the rod. However, hooking them by itself doesn't actually do them any damage.

More Fishing Tips

- A fishing rod can be used sixty-five times before it breaks.

- With a regular fishing rod, you have a 10 percent chance of catching junk and a 5 percent chance of catching treasure.

- Fishing lowers in durability when you hit a solid block, under water or on ground, or an entity.

- Endermen will teleport if you hook them but will still be hooked.

- If you are desperate for food, create your own pool of water from a 2×2 dug-out square. Fill it with water from the bucket of water you have stored, and fish in that!

- You can also fish in waterfalls.

You can make your own water hole to fish in, or even fish in a waterfall.

- You can use a fishing rod to pull a mob to a height. When the mob falls from a high enough level, it will be killed.

- Fish in a boat to get a break from mobs.

- You can fish inside and underground, but it will take about double the time to catch a fish.

- You don't have to stay absolutely still while fishing—you can move about thirty-five blocks from the bobber.

CHAPTER II

ENCHANTING AND POTIONS

Enchanting your weapons gives you an extra edge, which can mean the difference between life and death, and enchanting your mining tools lets you take home double the loot in half the time! There are a couple ways to enchant your tools, weapons, and armor. You can use an enchantment table or an anvil, or you can trade with a village priest. Except for the priest, enchanting costs experience points (XP).

Besides trading with a village priest, you enchant your tools and weapons through an enchantment table or an anvil.

An Enchanting Experience

Experience points are the main currency for enchanting, and you get XP (the floating green orbs) from doing things like killing mobs (other than baby animals, golems, bats, and villagers), mining (other than iron and gold), smelting and cooking with the furnace, fishing, trading, and breeding. Experience points fill up your experience bar, and when the bar is filled, you gain a new level. Then the bar is empty again and ready to fill for the next level. Above level 15, you need increasing XP at each level to reach the next. Experience points are only used for enchanting and the anvil. Make sure to pick up all the orbs you see, as any that aren't collected in five minutes disappear.

The floating green orbs that appear after you complete some activities, like killing a mob, add up to the experience levels you need to use the enchantment table and anvil. This experience bar is at level 74.

An Enchanting Village

You can buy enchanted items from villagers: armor from armorers, axes and swords from weapon smiths, picks from tool smiths, rods from fishermen, and books from librarians.

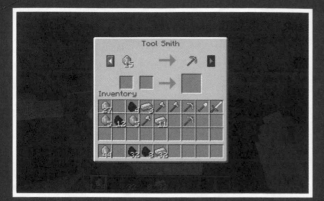

You can buy enchanted tools, weapons, armor, and more from villagers.

The Enchantment Table

Right-click an enchantment table to open the Enchant screen. Under the open book are two slots. In the left you place the item to be enchanted. In the right you place 1 to 3 lapis. On the right of the screen are three buttons that show three possible enchants for your item. The top button is an enchant you can get with 1 lapis, the middle will need 2 lapis, and the bottom will need 3. In addition to lapis, you will need to have a certain number of experience points to get an enchant. This is shown by the green number on each button. To know what the enchant will be and exactly what it will cost, mouse over the enchant button. It shows the enchant, the lapis amount, and the number of XP levels you will lose. You will only be shown one enchant per button however. Once you click the enchant button to place the enchant, you may get more!.

When you choose an enchantment with the enchantment table, you will only know one enchantment. You may actually end up getting two or more enchants.

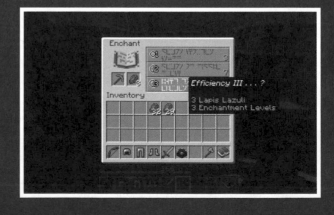

The more bookshelves that are placed around the enchantment table, the stronger the enchantment choices, and the more costly. You can put up to fifteen bookshelves around an enchantment table. There must be a block of space between the bookshelves and the enchantment table, and the bookshelves must be at the same height or one above the table. If you have placed so many bookshelves that you now don't have enough XP to buy at the high level of enchantments, you can disable the effect by placing torches on the side of the bookshelves facing the table.

To strengthen your enchantment table, place bookshelves around it, two blocks away. You'll see the magic symbols float from the shelves to the book on the enchantment table.

You can disable the strengthening effect of a bookshelf by placing a torch on it.

With an anvil you can:

- Combine two enchanted items to create an undamaged third item with both enchantments. The item in the left slot is the target, and the item in the right slot is "sacrificed." The two initial items must have compatible enchantments. If one of the initial items is damaged, then the cost will increase, but the total cost can't be more than 39 XP.

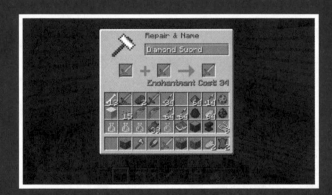

With an anvil, the two items you are repairing must have compatible enchantments.

- Enchant an item with the enchantment of an enchanted book. The enchanted book goes in the second slot.

You can enchant an item with an enchanted book. Hover over the rightmost slot to see what the final enchantment will bring.

- Repair an item with blocks of the same raw material it is made of. The raw material goes into the second slot.
- Rename an item. Renaming also costs XP. Renaming can also make it easier for you to find a favorite pickaxe!

Right-click to open an anvil. It will show your inventory, and there will be two slots you use. You place the item to repair in the left slot and the matching item (which you will sacrifice), or raw material (like iron) in the second. The repaired item shows in the slot at the far right. The repair will cost experience points. A tool tip will show the enchantments the repaired item will have. To see its durability, press F3+H. If both items you place are enchanted and the enchantments are compatible, the repaired item will have both enchantments.

Get More Experience

You get the most experience points from killing hostile mobs (especially those with armor), breaking a Bottle o'Enchanting (which you can get from a village priest), and from destroying mob spawners. You get a massive number of points for killing the Ender Dragon (12,000 XP) and fifty from killing a Wither. Fast ways to get more experience points quickly are mob experience (XP) farms and mining Nether quartz for experience. You can also breed animals quickly, killing and cooking their meat as you go.

- Don't repair an enchanted item on your crafting table. This will remove any enchantment. Use the anvil instead.

- The more you enchant an item, the more expensive in XP levels it gets. After a while (about 6 times) it will be too expensive to enchant.

- Reverse the order of two items in the anvil. This can sometimes make an enchant cheaper.

- Name tags are found in chests in dungeons and by fishing. You can rename them in the anvil and attach them to a mob.

- If you enchant books (or find them), you can build a library of books enchanted with different effects. Then you can choose to add a specific enchantment to an item by using the anvil.

- Anvils are damaged the more they are used. You can use an anvil about twenty-four times before it is very damaged and disappears.

When an anvil is very damaged and about to break, its surface looks spotted.

- An item can only have one type of protection enchantment and one type of damage enchantment at a time. It can't have two versions of the same enchantment, either.

Potions

Potions are very powerful. You brew them with a brewing station using rare ingredients. They grant you a specific power or ability, like breathing underwater, being fire resistant, or moving very fast for a certain amount of time. Witches sometimes drop potions when you kill them, but to have a reliable source of potions you will need to brew them yourself. To do this, you must have some ingredients you can only find in the Nether. You will need a blaze rod in order to craft the brewing stand. To get a blaze rod, you will need to kill a mob called the blaze, which lives in Nether fortresses.

In addition, most potions use Nether wart. You find Nether wart growing around staircases in Nether fortresses. It only grows on Soul Sand, also found in the Nether, but doesn't need light or water. Since you will need a supply of this, make your own farm by bringing back Nether wart and soul sand from a trip to the Nether.

For a potion-brewing setup, have at the ready your brewing stand, a water supply, a furnace for making glass bottles, and a supply of Nether warts.

To begin brewing potions, right-click the brewing station.

Primary Potions

Once you have filled bottles with water, you brew these with another ingredient to make a base or primary potion. Primary potions don't do anything themselves, but you brew them with other ingredients to create your final potion. You add Nether wart for the Awkward potion, glowstone dust for the Thick potion, and fermented spider eye for the Potion of Weakness. For the Mundane potion, you add one of the following: ghast tears, glistering melon, blaze powder, magma cream, sugar, or spider eye. You use redstone for the Mundane potion (extended time).

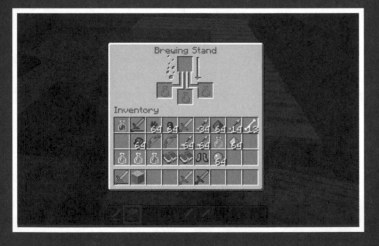

To make a potion, place glass bottles filled with water in the bottom slots and your added ingredient in the top slot. You don't have to fill all bottle slots, but if you don't you will waste ingredients.

Secondary Potions

Once you have a primary potion, you brew this with another ingredient for a secondary potion that you can use. The Awkward potion is the base for most secondary potions. With the Awkward potion, add magma cream for Fire Resistance, glistering melon for Healing, golden carrot for Night Vision, ghast tear for Regeneration, blaze powder for Strength, sugar for Swiftness, rabbit's foot for Leaping, and pufferfish for Water Breathing. For a Potion of Weakness, add the fermented spider eye to any of the base potions, and for a Potion of Poison, add spider eye to the Awkward potion.

Tertiary Potions

You can make new potions from these secondary potions. Add gunpowder to turn the potion into a splash potion, glowstone dust to make the potion twice as strong (and sometimes lose duration), and redstone to make the effect last twice as long. You can use fermented eye of spider to "corrupt" the effect, or make it do the opposite. For example, add the fermented eye of spider to a Potion of Swiftness to make it a Potion of Slowness.

More Potion Tips

- Combine a potion with gunpowder to turn it into a splash potion you can throw at your own feet or the feet of your enemy.

- To use a potion, you right-click with it in your hand. To see what potions you currently have active, open your inventory.

- For efficient brewing, always brew three bottles. One ingredient is enough to brew all three.

- You can add a single ingredient to three different types of potions. For example, you can brew gunpowder with a Potion of Poison, a Potion of Weakness, and a Potion of Harming in one brewing session.

- Using gunpowder for a splash potion makes it 25 percent less strong, and the shape of the bottle will change to a round shape with a handle, a bit like a grenade.

- Throwing a harming potion at a zombie or skeleton actually helps them heal (because they are undead to begin with!). Splash them with a healing potion instead.

- To fill a bottle, hold it and right-click a water source. Filling a water bottle from a water-filled cauldron will drain the cauldron by a third, so use a water supply you make yourself.

- The brewing station will show you the name of the final potion and its effect when you place a base potion and an ingredient into its slots.

- Because gathering the ingredients for potions is dangerous, use enchanting instead to help you while you hone your skills. When you are ready for trips back and forth from the Nether, you are ready for potions!

CHAPTER 12

UNDERSTANDING REDSTONE

Redstone is a powerful ore in Minecraft that allows you to make automatic contraptions like automatic sliding doors, elevators, and farms that harvest your wheat automatically.

An iron door is one of the simplest redstone contraptions. The device is the iron door, and it is activated (opened) by a power signal from the pressure plate on a neighboring block.

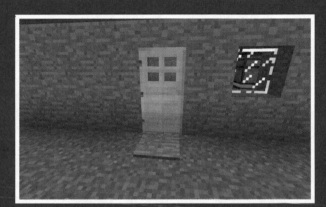

Redstone is a little bit like electricity. It is a power source, and you use redstone wire like an electric wire, sending power signals to an object or device to do something like open a door. A redstone contraption needs at least two things—redstone power source and the device itself. It can also have a third element for transmitting the power longer distances.

- **The device:** Redstone devices are items that respond to a redstone power signal by doing something. Devices include dispensers (which eject items), doors (which can be opened remotely), and pistons (which can move blocks).

- **The power source:** To get the device to react, you need to activate it with a power source. The power signal comes from a special item either made from redstone or programmed to give a signal. You can place the power source right next to the device to power it. Types of power sources include a redstone torch, a button, and a lever. A lever or button might seem like a type of device, but they actually produce a redstone signal that activates devices.

- **Power transmission:** If you want or need to place the power source further away from the device, you can use redstone wire to transmit the power. This means you can place a lever three blocks away from a piston and connect the two with redstone wire. Signals are also carried by two other items: comparators and repeaters.

A Simple Contraption: the Iron Door

A working iron door is one of the simplest redstone contraptions. Iron doors only open with a signal. Place your iron door in a wall of your home. Put a pressure plate directly in front of it. To open the door, stand on the pressure plate. Doing this makes the power source—the pressure plate—transmit a redstone signal to the door. The door—a device—is programmed to react to the signal by opening. However, if the door is an exterior door, don't use a pressure plate on the outside. A mob could stand on it by accident and get into your house. Put a button on the wall outside.

There are many types of power sources, devices, and ways to modify a power signal traveling along a wire. There are special rules that govern how each item acts and reacts. It gets pretty complicated, and creating redstone contraptions is one of the hardest things to do in Minecraft.

A great way to start working with and understanding redstone is to explore it and make machines, from simple to complex, in Creative mode. In Creative mode, you have access to all the types of blocks you need, without having to craft them. Put a power source next to a device that can be activated, like a lever next to a door, and see what happens. Search online for tutorials on building redstone mechanisms and follow them. First, learn what the different devices, power sources, and signal modifiers are.

Devices

- **Dispenser:** A dispenser ejects items in the same way a player drops items. However, if the item is a projectile, the dispenser will fire it. Some dispensed items are also activated (as when a player right-clicks an item). These items include minecarts (if there's a rail in front of the dispenser), boats (if there is water), TNT, bone meal, flint, steel, water buckets, and lava buckets. If you put these items in a dispenser they'll come out ready to go, so you can use dispensers to fill your moat with lava with a push of a button, remotely detonate TNT, or deploy a fleet of carts for your roller coaster from the control booth!

- **Doors:** These include iron doors, wood doors, fence gates, and trap doors. The only one of these that must have a power signal in order to work is an iron door, but you can power other doors, too. This way you can open your fence gates with a push of a button (they close quickly behind you to keep your animals from following), or open the doors inside your house with pressure plates. You can even make a trap door to drop you to the next floor with the flip of a switch!

- **Dropper:** Droppers drop items stored inside them to the floor or to a container that has an inventory, like a hopper or chest, in front of it.

- **Hopper:** A hopper transfers items between containers, including chests and minecarts. It can transfer items in its own small inventory of five items or items in a container placed above it. It transfers the items to containers placed below its output. Powering a hopper stops this activity.

- **Minecart rails:** These include powered rails, activator rails, and detector rails.

- **Note block:** When a note block receives a power signal or a player clicks it, it plays a musical note, F-sharp. You can right-click a note block to make it a higher pitch.

- **Piston and sticky piston:** When powered, a piston block expands to occupy two blocks, pushing the block in front of it one block away. A sticky piston can retract as well. You can use pistons to make all kinds of creations, like a castle drawbridge or a hidden cave door.

- **Redstone lamp:** A redstone lamp can be turned on by power. It is a little brighter than a torch, and it looks a bit more fashionable.

- **TNT:** You can detonate a block of TNT by powering it.

Redstone devices include doors, droppers, hoppers, power and activator rails, note blocks, pistons and sticky pistons, redstone lamps, and TNT.

Power Sources

Some power sources are always "on," or always transmitting power, and others need to be turned on like a switch. They provide power to themselves (the block space they are "in") and to the blocks they are attached to. Some power sources also power the blocks next to the block they are attached to. These include buttons, detector rails, levers, pressure plates, and trip wire hooks.

- **Redstone torch:** This provides power constantly, to itself and to the block above it, rather than the block it is placed on. However, if the block that the redstone torch is attached to gets powered or switched on separately by another block, the redstone torch will turn off.

- **Redstone block:** Like a redstone torch, redstone is always on. Unlike a redstone torch, it cannot be switched off. It cannot power the block above it, it only powers itself.

- **Lever:** In the "on" position, a lever provides power to the block it is attached to.

- **Button:** Pressing a stone button gives power for one second (a wood button 1.5 seconds) to itself and the block it is attached to. Wooden buttons can be pressed by arrows, which keep the button depressed.

- **Pressure plates:** Stone or wood pressure plates provide power for one second, or for the time an item is on it. Pressure plates are activated by players, mobs, or a minecart with a mob in it. Wooden plates can also be activated by arrows, fishing rod lures, any minecart, and any dropped items. A pressure plate powers the block beneath it.

- **Weighted pressure plates:** Gold and iron pressure plates provide an amount of power that depends on the weight of items dropped on them. Gold produces less power per item than iron.

- **Detector rail:** A detector rail provides a power signal when a minecart is on it. Detector rails are often used to switch the tracks a minecart is on.

- **Trip wire hooks:** Two trip wire hooks power the blocks they are attached to when the string that attaches them to each other is stood on or walked over (by a player, for example). Two trip wire hooks can be up to forty blocks apart.

- **Trapped chest:** You craft a trapped chest from a trip wire hook and chest. When the chest is opened, it produces a weak power to the block it is placed on and itself.

- **Daylight sensor:** Daylight sensors provide an amount of power that depends on the amount of daylight, so they are strongest at noon.

- **Containers:** Containers (with inventories) like brewing stands, chests, dispensers, droppers, furnaces, hoppers, and jukeboxes provide a power signal to a comparator. The signals they emit grow stronger the more items they contain, relative to the total amount they are able to store. This means that a container with twenty-seven slots but only three items will send a weaker signal than a container with five slots and three items.

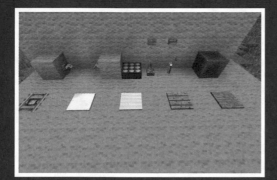

Redstone power sources transmit a redstone signal to a device. The signal may be temporary, as with a button, or constant, as with a redstone torch. They include redstone torches and redstone blocks, levers, buttons, pressure plates and weighted pressure plates, detector rails, daylight sensors, and trip wire hooks.

Transmitting Power

To connect a power source that is a block or more away from the device, you will need to use redstone wire. You can modify the redstone signal with a repeater or a comparator.

- **Redstone wire:** Redstone wire carries power from a power source for fifteen blocks. The signal weakens as it travels. You can tell redstone wire is carrying power if it lights up and is sparkling. The redstone wire gives power to the block beneath it and the block that the end of the wire is attached to.

(Redstone "occupies" the block above the block that it is sitting on.)

- **Redstone repeater:** Redstone repeaters allow redstone wire to carry the signal longer than fifteen blocks. A repeater increases the power signal to its original strength and lets it travel another fifteen blocks. Repeaters also cause a delay in the signal. You can set the delay to .1, .2, .3, or .4 seconds. Power can only pass through a repeater in one direction, from the back to the front, marked by a faint triangle or arrow.

- **Comparator:** A comparator looks a bit like a repeater but it does something different. It compares the signal coming to it from the back to the signal coming to it from the side. (The front is marked the same way as a repeater, with an arrow.) If the signal from the back is greater than the signal from the side, it will send the back signal power out the front; otherwise, it will send no signal. A comparator can also act in a "subtract" mode, which you activate by right-clicking it. In subtract mode, it compares the two signals, then subtracts the amount of power coming from the side and then sends the rest forward. If the side power is greater than the back, no signal is sent.

In changing the signal being transmitted, you use redstone wire (to carry the signal for fifteen blocks), redstone repeaters (to help the signal carry longer than fifteen blocks), and comparators (to modify a signal based on a second signal's input).

Timing Is Everything

One thing to be aware of when building complicated contraptions is that many of these blocks react with small delays in timing, called ticks. For example a redstone torch takes one tick (.1 seconds) to change from on to off. This means that complicated machines may not work as you expect, because there are too many delays. You need to be careful about timing, and if you are having a problem, you can research the items you are using online to see what advanced features and side effects they have that may be causing the problem. Creating machines and circuits with redstone gets to be very advanced—like studying electronics. You can read more about all of these elements online. A great place to start is the Minecraft wiki, at minecraft.gamepedia.com.

Powered Blocks

Most solid blocks, like cobblestone, that you can't see through can be powered. A powered block doesn't transmit power to the blocks next to it, but it can activate a device it is next to. This is what happens when you push a button on a block next to an iron door. See-through blocks, like glass or leaves, typically can't be powered.

Cobblestone Piston Doors

Pistons and sticky pistons are used in many redstone contraptions because they move the block immediately in front of them. They are used in contraptions to harvest farm crops, kill mobs, move elevators, and make sliding doors. Follow these steps for a set of automatic sliding piston doors.

(a) Place four cobblestone blocks, two wide and two high, to make the doors.

(b) On the side of the door, place two sticky pistons stacked on top of each other, one block away from the door. (When you place a piston, the moving slab faces you.)

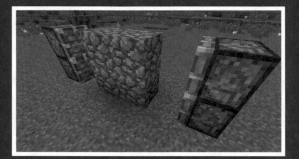

Create two cobblestone doors out of four cobblestone blocks. Add two sets of two sticky pistons, one block away on each side.

(c) Place a redstone torch with a cobblestone block on top, on the other side of the two sticky piston stacks. The redstone torch activates the bottom piston. It also powers the cobblestone above it, which activates the top sticky piston.

Power the pistons. The bottom one is activated by a redstone torch. The top piston is activated by the same redstone torch signal, passed through the cobblestone block above the torch.

These three steps create a piston door that is shut, because the power from the redstone torch—which is always on—keeps the pistons extended. But you need to have the doors open to get through them, of course! So you need a way to power off the redstone torch powering the pistons. Luckily, whenever a redstone torch has power sent to it, it turns off! To do this, you can use pressure plates that will send a power signal over redstone wire to the redstone torches. The four pressure plates (two on either side of the door) will be placed two blocks away from the doors.

(d) Dig two trenches two blocks deep on each side to connect the side of the redstone torch with the pressure plates. However, at the redstone torch, you will need to place one block as a step to reach it. This is because redstone wire can't climb up more than one block at a time, so you use stepped blocks to raise the wire. The trench must be two blocks deep, because redstone needs a free block above it in order to work. (You can use a slab in place of a block to cover redstone, as this leaves space for the redstone to work.)

(e) When the trenches are dug, place redstone wire along them from one end to the other.

Dig trenches to run redstone wire from one end to the other.

(f) On both sides of the door, replace the empty blocks directly in front of the doors with wood planks or another flooring material, and place your pressure plates on these.

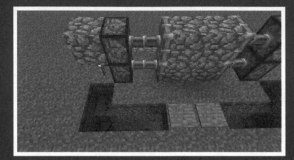

Add dirt blocks in front of the doors and stone pressure plates along these.

You should now be able to pass through the doors. As you walk on the pressure plates, they give power to the redstone wire beneath them that travels to the sticky pistons and turns them off. This makes the doors open. By the time you pass through the doors, the pressure plates turn off, closing the doors. Now you can cover up the trenches and wiring with any building blocks you like. Remember that you must leave a block of space above each block with placed redstone wire. If the redstone wire is traveling up the side of a block, it is the top of that block that needs a full block of space above it.

This is the finished door, with the sliding door mechanisms completely covered up.

CHAPTER 13

RAILWAYS

Whether you need to traffic loads of ore from your mines back to your base, or you just want a quick way to travel to all the villages you are saving, minecart railways are a perfect way to speed up your journeys. Except for horses (and flying in Creative mode), they're the fastest way to get around. You can build them up, around, or through mountains and down to the bottommost mines, cross lakes, and stop along the way at stations you can trick out any way you like. You aren't safe from mobs while you're traveling though. Even a sheep can get in the way and derail you. The safest railways are underground, in lit corridors that mobs can't spawn in, or elevated. If you are building an elevated railway, make sure to keep it lit and well away from trees and other blocks that mobs can jump from.

Build an elevated railway to steer clear of mobs, but make sure to keep it lit!

Types of Minecarts

As well as the standard minecart you ride in, you can also create a powered minecart (a minecart with a furnace), which can push carts in front of it; a storage minecart (cart with a chest); and a hopper minecart (a cart with a hopper). Hopper minecarts gather items on the track or can be loaded from other containers. Minecarts don't attach to each other, but one can push the others in front.

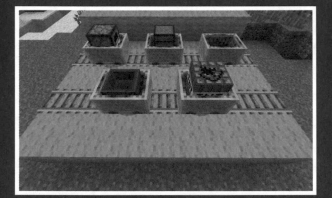

As well as the regular minecart you can hop in yourself, there's a powered minecart, storage minecart, hopper minecart, and TNT minecart.

Types of Rails

Along with the regular rails, there are three types of rails that perform specific duties:

- **Powered rails:** Activate these with a redstone torch or they will bring the cart to a stop. A redstone torch will activate the powered rail it is attached to and up to eight additional powered rails following it. Powered rails can also be activated by detector rails, powered redstone wire, a lever, or by being placed on a redstone block.

- **Detector rails:** Detector rails act like a pressure plate. They give out a power signal when a cart is over them to their neighboring blocks. You can use these to power powered rails, activate note blocks to signal a train is coming, activate dispensers to drop items or shoot arrows, or switch tracks at a T junction.

- **Activator rails:** When powered, these can do two things: activate or deactivate a hopper minecart, or activate a TNT minecart.

The four types of rails are regular rails, powered rails, detector rails, and activator rails.

Simple Railway System

You can easily build a one-track railway system with stops on the way and two simple endpoints. Power your railway starts by digging a 2×1 hole and using powered rails. The very last rail at the endpoint should have a button that you press to get going.

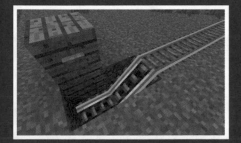

This simple endpoint stop uses two powered rails and a button to power the last powered rail.

For in-between stops, dig a 2×1 hole that has two powered rails in the hole, also powered with a button. This will bring your cart to a stop, then you press the button to move forward in the direction you are going.

The simplest in-between stop has two powered rails and a button.

Another simple in-between stop uses a raised 2×1 platform with regular rails on top. At either end of the platform, place two powered rails leading to the platform and, next to these, detector rails. Connect buttons with redstone wire to the rising powered rails on either side. The detector rails power your movement up to the platform, and the buttons power you forward. (If your button doesn't seem to be working, make sure you are on the powered rail that is sloping. You can adjust your position slightly by pressing W.)

Another type of in-between stop uses a platform, four powered rails, two detector rails, and two buttons. Here, the buttons are connected to the powered rails by redstone wire.

Build a fantastic roller coaster by using cobblestone, wood planks, or other blocks to make your base for the rails. Place rails on the ramps, adding plenty of powered rails to help your minecart go up slopes. End the rollercoaster where you started. To build a simple stop, place two powered rails, the first on a descending block and the second on a level block. Place a button on a wall beside the descending block. When your cart reaches the descending block, it will brake. You can start it forward again by pressing the button. (You must be on the descending block while pressing the button.)

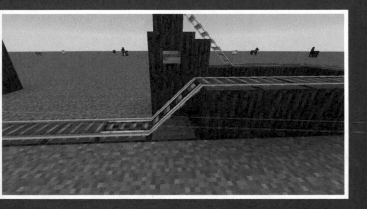

This rollercoaster uses another type of stop. Notice the button powers the sloping powered rail.

There are two main rules for how powering a powered rail helps a stationary minecart start moving again.

(1) If there is a block at one end of the powered rail, the minecart will be moved in the opposite direction.

(2) If the powered rail is on a slope, the minecart will be moved down the slope.

Rails aren't just for transporting ore. Build a rollercoaster high in the sky.

Full Speed Ahead

Some Minecraft players timed the speeds and effects of powered rails. Their results showed that for full speed on a level surface (for an occupied cart), place a powered rail every thirty-four blocks. Other studies say to put two powered rails every thirty-seven blocks. Going up a slope, put a powered rail every four blocks. For an unoccupied cart, you'll need a powered rail every seven blocks. Uphill, place powered rails every two blocks for occupied carts and every block for unoccupied carts.

More Tips on Rails

- Minecarts move faster when a player is in them than when they are empty.

- Use a pickaxe to break up rails fastest.

- Occasionally, a curved rail that is placed correctly will look like it is curving in the wrong direction. Test it with a cart to see if it is working.

- Your minecart will travel faster on "diagonal" rails—rails that curve in one direction for one block, then another, continuously.

Curving rails left and right with each block creates diagonal rails. Your cart will travel in a straight line down the diagonal, with increased speed.

- At intersections where tracks cross each other but aren't curved, minecarts will always take whichever direction is downhill. If all directions are level, then the cart will turn either to the south or to the east.

- You can also put TNT in a minecart and activate the blast with a powered activator rail, fire, lava, a collision, or by dropping over three blocks.

- Only regular rails can be used at a curve or a T junction.

- You can't place a powered rail at a curve.

CHAPTER 14

GETTING CREATIVE

The block is the basic building unit in Minecraft, and Minecraft blocks are designed to be stacked, combined, and rearranged in an endless number of ways to create just about anything you can think of. While you can build working devices, contraptions, railways, clothes, tools, and other useful things, you can also use blocks just to be creative. Make two-dimensional pixel art with Minecraft's colored blocks.

Make pixel art with Minecraft's colored blocks.

Build the Minecraft version of your own home, create a medieval castle, or sculpt a mountain into Godzilla. Minecraft players have built (singly or in teams) incredible models of real-life palaces, cities, and national monuments, from the Empire State Building to the Taj Mahal. If building is your thing, there's lots you can do!

Creative Home Design

Your first Minecraft home was probably a simple square or a hole dug into a mountain. But if you have an architectural streak, there's no limit to the styles and sizes of homes and buildings you can create, with all of the building and textured blocks the game offers. To get started improving your house design:

- Use two types of contrasting blocks for your main structures. You can use one of the block types for corners and edges, as accent. For a modern look, try stone (not cobblestone) and light wood planks. For a country look, use cobblestone and wood planks. Mix light and dark wood, planks and raw wood. Bring in colored walls by using stained (dyed) clay, like a green clay, and pair it with sandstone.

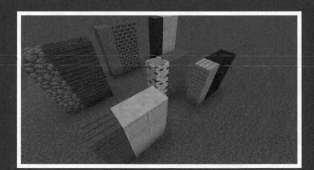

One way to make a house stand out is to use contrasting blocks and textures.

For a great, simple look, use two different types of blocks. This house uses the stone block and the dark oak wood block as well as leaf blocks for edging. You can use slabs to build up the slopes of a roof.

With dyed clay blocks, you can make very colorful buildings and structures.

- Add details: chimneys, hedges made from leaf blocks, ponds, fountains, and pathways. Use slabs to build up peaked roofs.

Add chimneys, hedges, and landscaping details to your homes.

- Get inspiration! Look online and in books for houses and styles you'd like to build. Build a towering castle with turrets, a pagoda, a treehouse with winding treetop paths, a modern beachside home, or massive military barracks!

- Leave the tiny 1×1 windows behind. Add wide windows, floor to ceiling windows, even skylights. In traditional houses, use trap doors for shutters.

- Use slabs to make different levels of floor inside.

Players have discovered many inventive ways to use Minecraft blocks for home design, furniture, and décor. There are some built-in home decoration items: paintings, carpet, flowerpots, glass panes, and item frames. When you place a painting on a wall, you'll randomly get one of twenty-six Minecraft paintings, in sizes 1×1 up to 4×4. The block where you place the painting will be the painting's bottom left corner.

Even though Minecraft doesn't include chairs and table and other furniture, players have been using existing blocks to add furniture and more to their homes. Experiment with combining blocks with fences, fence gates, signs, stair blocks, slabs, pressure plates, trap doors, pistons, glowstone, dyed wool, glass, and buttons. A stair block with two signs on its sides is a chair!

Some classic combinations are:

- Chairs and sofas: Use stairs or slabs, with signs or trap doors for arms.

- Tables: Use fence block with pressure plates above.

- Lamps: Fence block with glowstone, surrounded by trap doors.

- Fireplace: Place Netherrack within nonflammable blocks like stone, and light for an inside roaring fire. (Make sure the fire is not within 2 blocks of flammable material like wood.)

Make sofas and chairs from stairs, and use trapdoors and signs for arms. Use a slab for a coffee table. You can make a floor lamp with fencing, glowstone, and trap doors, and a TV from black wool and a painting.

Dyeing for Color

There are sixteen dyes you can make in Minecraft, and you can use the dyes to color wool, sheep, hardened clay, leather armor, banners, and glass. Some dyes you make by placing a flower of the same color on a crafting grid: Rose Red, Orange, Dandelion Yellow, Light Blue (orchid), Magenta (lilac, allium), Pink, Light Gray (white tulip, oxeye daisy, azure bluet). For Cactus Green, smelt a cactus; for Lapis Lazuli dye (a deep blue), use the lapis lazuli ore; and for White, use bone meal. Use a squid ink sac for Black and cocoa beans for Cocoa Bean (brown). You can also make some four other dyes: Lime (cactus green and bone meal), Gray (bone meal and ink sac), Cyan (cactus green and lapis lazuli), Purple (lapis lazuli and red). For a constant supply of dyed wool, dye a sheep. You can also combine dyes with glass for stained glass and with hardened clay (created by smelting clay or from the Mesa biome) for stained clay.

You can make sixteen dyes using plants and other items, and they can be used to color wool (and sheep), glass, and hardened clay.

Fireworks!

Make colorful explosions in the sky with fireworks. Fireworks can only be crafted—they are not in the Creative mode inventory. To create an exploding firework, first make a colored firework star using gunpowder and a dye. Add a diamond in the crafting screen to add trails or glowstone dust to add a twinkle. You can also change the shape of the explosion from a sphere. For a larger sphere, add a fire charge; for a star shape, add a gold nugget. Add a feather for a burst and any mob head for a creeper head shape. Then, to make the final firework rocket, combine your fireworks star with one paper and one gunpowder. Add one or two more gunpowder for greater height and more firework stars for more explosions! Set these off outside by right-clicking to place them.

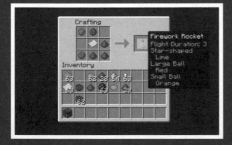

Create fireworks with firework stars, gunpowder, and paper. What you add to a firework star determines its shape, color, and special effects like trails, and you can combine multiple stars into one rocket.

Consider Creative Mode

If you are planning an extensive build, and the glory of battling mobs isn't a priority, work in Creative mode. In Creative mode, you have access to all of Minecraft's blocks, from cyan wool to decorative mob heads. You don't need tools—you can destroy blocks with your hand or any other item except a sword. And you can fly, placing blocks anywhere in the sky to make floating castles and sky-high mob farms. You won't get hungry or be damaged if you fall, so you have all the time you need to make whatever you want.

Also in Creative mode:

- You can use the search screen in your inventory to find items.

- If you are destroying a large area of dirt or stone, for example, use a dirt or stone block to do it. This way, you can easily replace a space you didn't mean to make with the block in your hand.

- You can use your mouse middle key as a pick block. By middle-clicking a block, you place it in your hotbar and your hand.

- Empty buckets stay empty, and water and lava buckets stay filled.

- You have access to Creative mode—only blocks— the sponge block (decorative) and spawn eggs, which you place on the ground to spawn mobs like sheep or creepers.

- When it rains, use commands to stay in daylight and clear weather: Use **/weather clear 10000** to stop the rain for 10,000 seconds and **/time set day** to go back to daylight.

Minecraft Music

You can play a tune by tuning note blocks in a sequence and activating them through redstone power. You make a note block a half-note higher each time you right-click it. An un-clicked note block makes an F-sharp note, so to make it sound a G, click once. Once you reached the highest note possible (after two octaves), it returns to emitting the lowest note. You can change the tone of the sound by changing the block beneath the note block. Most blocks, including dirt, produce piano tones. Glass blocks produce clicks. Sand and gravel produce a snare drum sound. Wood blocks produce a bass guitar sound and stone blocks produce a bass drum sound.

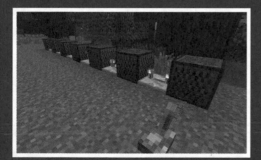

Connect tuned note blocks together with repeaters and activate to make a tune.

For example, the opening seven notes for "Twinkle Twinkle Little Star" are G, G, D, D, E, E, D. Set up seven note blocks in a row, with one repeater (pointing to the next note in sequence) between each. Right-click each repeater three times for the maximum signal delay. Then, tune each of the seven notes. For a G, right-click it once; for a D, right-click eight times; and for an E, right-click ten times. Power the first G note block with a lever and redstone wire. Flip the lever, and you'll get the tune!

Music on a Jukebox

There's a jukebox in Minecraft you can craft with a diamond in the middle of eight wood planks. To find music discs to play, you'll need to do some exploring, as only a couple of discs can be found in dungeon chests.

To get more music discs, you'll have to trick a skeleton into killing a creeper. One way to do this is to first damage the creeper, but not kill it, with three blows from a stone sword. This means that a skeleton can then kill it with one arrow. Lead the creeper until you can get it into position between you and a skeleton. Then walk backward, keeping the creeper between you and the skeleton. Another trick is to first lure the skeleton into one end of a ditch and a damaged creeper into the other end.

If you can get a skeleton to shoot a creeper, the creeper will drop a music disc.

CHAPTER 15

THE NETHER

The Nether is Minecraft's fiery underworld. There is no day or night, no flowers, ponds, or villagers—it is a dark world lit by lava and flames. The terrain is dangerous, with seas of lava and high, treacherous cliffs. The Nether is teeming with its own dangerous mobs: zombie pigmen, enormous firebombing ghasts, whirling blazes, creepy magma cubes, and Wither skeletons.

The Nether landscape: columns and seas of lava, floating islands of Netherrack, raging fires, and plenty of hostile mobs.

So why go there? It is only place you can find the rarest of Minecraft's materials. There is glowstone to make redstone lamps, Nether quartz to make redstone comparators and daylight sensors, and Nether wart for potions. The items dropped made by Nether mobs you kill are especially valuable. Magma cream and ghast tears are used for potions. So are blaze rods, which you also need to find to lead you to the End. And if you want to accomplish all of Minecraft's achievements, including getting to the End, you will need to visit and raid a Nether fortress.

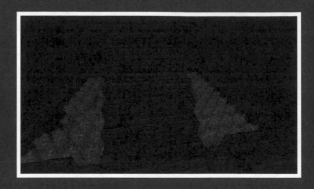

You can find Nether wart growing at the bottom of fortress staircases.

To visit the Nether, you must construct a portal of at least ten obsidian blocks surrounding a three-block-high, two-block-wide empty space. Once built, you activate the portal by igniting the center space with flint and steel or a fire charge.

You only need ten obsidian blocks to make a portal, but you can make portals as big as 23×23.

Stand in the portal to be teleported. When the animation stops, step out into the Nether. Watch out: a portal can spawn near or over lava, a tiny ledge suspended in midair, and other dangerous places. Secure your portals with a cobblestone wall to keep out the mobs on either side. Even better, create a roofed base of operations around your Nether portal. Cobblestone can withstand the fireballs that ghasts throw.

Be Prepared!

Make sure you are equipped at least with a full set of armor, as well as potions, enchanted weapons, and tools to help you survive and fight. You'll need your swords, bows, and pickaxe. You'll need plenty of cobblestone to make bridges across the lakes of lava, as well as gravel and a shovel for pillar jumping up and down cliffs. You can also take ladders to help you climb. Take material to build another portal in case yours is destroyed. As with mining, bring chests to store loot, wood to make a crafting table, and iron to make new weapons and tools. Don't forget food!

Find the Fortress

Your main priority in the Nether is to find a Nether fortress, but it's difficult to see well in the dim light. To help, you can use a Potion of Night Vision or change your video settings in your game options to maximize the screen's brightness and the render distance. Look for flat, dark, tall areas of Nether fortress walls that are straight up and down instead of the jagged profiles of cliffs. Nether fortresses can have long walkways and tall windows. They are placed along north/south lines, so one tactic is to just head either east or west to find one. Compasses don't work in the Nether, so use your F3 Debug screen to get your direction. Use torches or Jack o'Lanterns to mark your path.

You can recognize a Nether fortress by the vertical dark shapes in the distance.

Bring plenty of cobblestone to build bridges over lava.

Once you get to your Nether fortress, you have several main goals:

- Locate chests and their valuable loot.

- Find Nether wart that grows around the bottom of staircases.

- Find a blaze spawner so you can kill multiple blazes and get the blaze rods they drop.

Fighting the Nether Mobs

Blaze

Use snowballs against a blaze, as they cause three points of damage each and can give you some time to get close and use your sword. Build a small barricade to hide behind, popping out to damage them as they get close.

It can be hard getting close to a blaze to kill it and dangerous to take time loading arrows. Try snowballs—they deal three points of damage—as you get close with your sword.

Zombie Pigmen

Zombie pigmen are neutral unless you attack one. Then the pig-man, and any pigmen nearby, will attack you as a horde if they can see you. Avoid fighting them, or, if you must, stay more than sixteen blocks away and shoot with your bow. They are not very clever, and a wall can hold them at bay. You can push them off a cliff without provoking them. Baby zombie pigmen are faster than the adults, so they are a bit more dangerous.

Zombie pigmen are neutral until attacked. If you attack one, though, a host of others will join to pursue you.

Ghasts

You can use any tool to smack back a ghast's fireballs. You can influence the direction by using an arrow or snowball to hit the fireball. Move side to side to prevent the ghast from getting a good aim at you. Fire your arrows at their tentacles. One arrow from an enchanted bow can kill them. They only have ten health points, so if you can bring one close, you can kill it in one or two blows from a sword.

You can use any tool to smack back a ghast's fireball.

Magma Cubes

Magma cubes are like slime but more dangerous. Use a bow to kill the big ones first and move back as it spawns smaller ones. Wait to use your sword on the small ones.

A magma cube is the Nether version of slime.

Wither Skeletons

Keep your distance so you can use a bow and arrow. Because a Wither skeleton is over two blocks high, create a barricade with a 2×1 hole you can escape and fight through.

Wither skeletons are over two blocks high, so you can place barricades and doors that only you can pass through.

- If you get completely lost, you can create another portal to take you back to the Overworld.

- Mobs can travel through a portal, and items can be thrown through a portal. Storage minecarts, powered minecarts, empty minecarts, and boats can also go through a portal.

- If you are bringing back Nether wart for growing, don't forget the Soul Sand it grows in. You can usually find Soul Sand near lava.

- One way to store your Nether loot is in an Ender chest. An Ender chest is an interdimensional chest, and wherever you build the chest you will have access to the same materials. So you can build an Ender chest in the Nether to hold your loot. To access the same loot from the Overworld, just build another Ender chest. An Ender chest is built with eight obsidian blocks and one Eye of Ender.

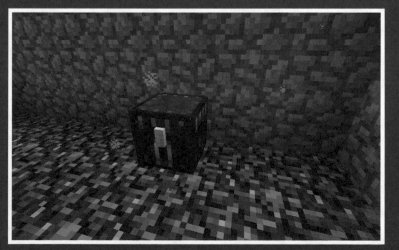

All of the contents you place in an Ender chest are available in any realm, wherever you place another Ender chest.

- Bring golden and enchanted golden apples. Either will help regenerate you, and an enchanted golden apple also provides fire resistance.

- Since your chances of dying in the Nether are high, leave very valuable items at home in a chest.

- Maps can help you in the Nether. Even though they don't show any landmarks, they do show you where you are in relationship to the center of the map, which is the point you first use the map. So if you start a map at your Nether portal, you will be able to see the direction you must go to get back there.

A map in the Nether only shows you the bedrock ceiling, but it will show you where you are from the map's center.

- Try to kill ghasts over land so you can gather their tears.

- Don't bring water or beds. Water will sizzle up so you can't use it, and trying to sleep in a bed will explode the bed.

- You can use a fishing rod to catch a ghast, bring it close over land, and attack with a sword.

Portal Networks

Because traveling one block in the Nether is the same as traveling eight blocks in the Overworld, you can create a network of portals in the Nether that allow you to travel far distances in the Overworld. The most reliable way of doing this is creating the connected portals by hand. First you create the Overworld portal at coordinates x, y, and z. Then travel to the Nether and create a portal there that will bring you back to where you built the first portal in the Overworld. Do this by finding the spot with the coordinates x/8 (the value of x divided by 8), y, and z. The height axis, y, is matched as closely as possible in Overworld/Nether mapping. You may have to dig in the Netherrack, create bridges over lava, or create a platform to build your Nether portal on. In the Nether, you can create paths, stairs, and bridges between your Nether portals, along with signs so you can remember which portals lead where. This doesn't always work exactly as you plan, and a portal may end up in a different area than you expect. You may need to experiment as you go.

More Portal Tips

- In Survival mode, you have about four seconds in the portal while you are being teleported. During this time, you can change your mind and step back into the Overworld.

- If you create a second portal close to another in the Overworld (within about 1,024 blocks in the Overworld), the second portal will transport you to the same Nether portal as the first. In the Nether, the distance to maintain separate portals is 128 blocks.

- You can create a portal without needing a diamond pickaxe to mine obsidian. Instead, you create
the obsidian by creating waterfalls against a wall,
then pouring lava from a bucket onto the blocks
where the obsidian frame should be.

You can create a portal by making waterfalls and pouring lava onto the
blocks where obsidian should be.

CHAPTER 16

THE END AND BEYOND

Although Minecraft is a sandbox game designed for endless exploration and play, it does have a "Campaign mode," with a victory to achieve called "The End." To finish the game and win, you have to go to the End, of course. The End is a special realm in the same way the Nether is. It is an island, floating in the void, populated by Endermen and the Ender Dragon. Once there, your only task is to defeat the Ender Dragon, which is extremely difficult. If you defeat the Dragon, Minecraft shows you the end credits along with a poem called "The End."

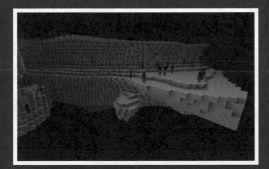

The End is an island floating in the void, where Endermen and the Ender Dragon live.

Eyes of Ender

In order to get to the end and defeat the dragon, you must have Eyes of Ender. Eyes of Ender are used to find End portals that transport you to the End. End portals are found in underground structures called strongholds. However, the End portal is broken, and to repair it you will need up to twelve more Eyes of Ender. The highly prized Eyes of Ender are crafted by combining blaze powder with Ender pearls, or you may be able to trade for them with village priests. To find an End portal, throw the Eye of Ender in the air. Do this in an area where you have a good view. If you are far from the End portal, the eye will float off in the direction of the portal and drop so you can pick it up again. Repeat this action until the Eye of Ender drops straight onto the ground in front of you. (You may need three or four eyes to finish this task.) This means the End portal is below you. When you dig, create a spiraling staircase or a ladder shaft so you don't stray too far from the spot.

Throw an Eye of Ender and follow its direction to locate a stronghold.

The End Portal

The End portal is in a room and is placed over a pool of lava. There is also a silverfish spawner you will need to destroy, along with any silverfish. Don't destroy any of the blocks the portal is created with, though—you can't replace them. Go ahead and add your Eyes of Ender to any of the portal blocks that are missing them. Once all eyes are in place, the portal will activate.

A stronghold's portal room contains a broken portal over a pool of lava and a silverfish spawner.

Fix and activate the portal by adding Eyes of Ender.

Strongholds

Strongholds are pretty interesting places you should look for even if you don't care about the Ender Dragon. Each Minecraft world you create has a maximum of three strongholds, usually between 640 and 1,152 blocks from X, Y, and Z coordinates of 0, 0, 0. They are a maze of dungeon-like rooms. In addition to the End portal room, these include rooms with fountains, libraries with bookshelves, and storage rooms with chests. But beware of digging through the walls, as this can release and provoke silverfish hiding in blocks.

Strongholds are a maze of rooms that include libraries, storage rooms with chests, and fountain rooms.

The only way to get back from the End is to win or be killed and respawn. Since you may need to try several times to kill the Ender Dragon, set up a base at the stronghold, sleeping in a bed so that if you are killed, you respawn there. That way you'll have everything you need (crafting tables, furnaces, iron, wood, etc.) to take another trip to the End. You may even want to plan on taking an exploratory trip to the End, to survey it and plan what you will need, then die to come back to your new spawn point in the End portal room.

You will want to take diamond and, if possible, enchanted armor and weapons. Bring at least two stacks of arrows if you don't have an infinity enchantment. Use Sharpness enchantment for your sword and Feather Fall for your boots. Bring a pumpkin and helmet, gravel and a shovel for pillar jumping (or ladders), and a pickaxe for digging. Bring a stack of obsidian to build bridges that the dragon can't destroy.

The End Itself

The End is a small island with columns of obsidian, hordes of Endermen, and the massive Ender Dragon. You will spawn on a ledge of obsidian, and the ledge may be some distance from the dragon's island. You may need to build or dig your way to the island.

Defeating the Dragon

The dragon is a very powerful boss mob that can wipe out half of your health with one blow. It is called a boss mob because it is programmed with more complex actions and reactions than regular mobs. When it is near you, your display shows the dragon's health bar.

You can wear a pumpkin so you don't look at any Endermen by accident and provoke them. Next, locate the Ender crystals on towers. These help the dragon heal quickly, and you must destroy these. Use a bow and arrow to do this, because the crystals explode when they are destroyed. You may need to build a pillar to get high enough to destroy some crystals. Keep some distance from them or use enchanted diamond armor.

To kill the dragon, wait until it is flying right at you, then aim your arrow at its head. This causes the most damage. With the pumpkin on your head, you only need to worry about the dragon. It may take some time to damage the dragon enough to kill it, so have plenty of arrows. When the dragon dies, it explodes. Beneath it is an exit portal with a dragon egg on top. Take the exit portal to view the end credits and poem and get back to your last spawn point in the Overworld!

Fire at the dragon's head to cause the most damage.

More End Tips

- If you don't want to use a pumpkin to avoid Endermen, build an Iron Golem army to help kill Endermen.

- When you hit the dragon and do damage, it flies away for a little bit. You can use this time to regroup or run somewhere else.

- The Ender Dragon can topple cobblestone, so bring obsidian to build shelters and bridges.

- The dragon egg doesn't do anything, but it is a trophy of your achievement. However, it is difficult to retrieve. One way is to first click on the egg with a tool to make it teleport a few blocks away. Then dig just one block out, two spaces below the egg. Place a torch in this space. Then knock out the block just below it to make the egg drop again as a resource. Now you can pick it up. To prevent the dragon egg initially teleporting into the exit portal, cover the exit portal with blocks temporarily.

- You can teleport with an Ender pearl, but it will cost you five points of damage. Throw the Ender pearl by right-clicking and you will teleport where it lands.

Beyond the End

Once you reach the End, that's not it! There's one last enemy you can vanquish: the Wither. And of course, there is no end to the games you can play, worlds you can visit, maps you can explore, and machines you can build. There's a vast community of miners ready with suggestions and tips for new ways to play and have fun.

Create and Destroy a Wither

The Wither is a three-headed boss mob that can only be created by a player. To fill the achievement of spawning a Wither, you must first kill the Ender Dragon. To build a Wither, you must stack Soul Sand in a T, similar to making a golem. Then you place three wither skeleton skulls on the top of the T. When the Wither is spawned, it flashes, grows, and creates a large explosion. Run away as soon as you create the Wither to avoid being damaged or killed. You will want to be using enchanted diamond armor and weapons, as well as potions. To fight the Wither, use bows as you approach, then drink a strength potion and use your enchanted diamond sword to kill it at close range.

Right after you create a Wither, it flashes, then explodes, before enlarging to its final shape.

One tactic that some players use to defeat the Wither is to create a small room at the top of the Nether, with bedrock as its ceiling. Here you can create the Wither on a piston and activate the piston to raise the Wither's heads into the bedrock. Once the Wither has exploded, it is still stuck in the bedrock, and you can kill it with your sword. Because the Wither creates so much damage by hurling exploding Wither skulls, you might want to fight it in the End, after you've defeated the dragon, of course.

Build a Beacon

Beacons are blocks that shoot up columns of light and can be powered to give you special powers. To build a beacon you must have a Nether star, which is dropped when you kill the Wither. It is therefore one of the rarest Minecraft blocks. It must be built on a pyramid of iron, gold, emerald, or diamond blocks (not ore). The smallest base it can be built on (level 1) is a 3×3 block, and the largest it can be built on is a 9×9 base pyramid (level 4).

There are four sizes of beacon you can make, using gold, emerald, iron, and diamond blocks. Larger beacons deliver more powerful effects.

Beacons are great for making a visible landmark. Even better, you can add an iron or gold ingot or an emerald or diamond to it to gain special powers, some of which are the same as abilities given by potions. The special powers are haste, speed, jump boost, strength, resistance, and regeneration. The special powers only affect you if you are within a certain distance of the beacon: within twenty blocks of a level 1 beacon, going up to fifty blocks for level 4. Each level gives you increasing choices of powers that can be granted. Level 1 beacons only offer speed and haste, while Level 4 beacons can give you two powers at the same time. Once you've built a beacon, right-click it to access its activation screen to add the iron, gold, emerald, or diamond and activate its powers.

Maps and Multiplayer

Yes, there's even more to do! Although you can play endlessly in singleplayer mode, you can also play user-created maps and try multiplayer Minecraft. To play multiplayer you will need access to a server, or you will need a home network to set up your own server. If you are joining a server you will need to understand the risks and requirements involved in this. It's best to have an experienced friend or parent show you the ropes, both with joining a server or with setting up a server for you and your friends to play on. In multiplayer, you can chat with other players and form groups to build amazing cities, houses, and castles, or just survive together. An easier way to set up a multiplayer world is through Minecraft Realms. This is a Mojang service that lets you set up an online world and share it with other players, but it does require a monthly fee.

You can also play specially created maps that are built by other users to test your abilities. Many maps can be played in singleplayer mode. Some maps use game mods (modification applications). You need to be sure you are running the same version of the game that the map uses, as well as any mods needed.

There are several types of maps you can play. Adventure maps give you a quest to perform and survival maps are designed to test your fighting and survival skills. There are also puzzle maps, which give you logical puzzles to solve, and parkour maps. Parkour maps test your agility running and jumping between platforms, columns, and ledges. There are also creative maps, which have amazing and creative builds for you to enjoy. Once you've played lots of maps, you may have your own idea for a map to create!

Caution
It is pretty easy to mess up your version of Minecraft—even your computer—when you download and install unofficial files

like mods and maps, so it is best to have someone experienced with this read through the instructions and help you, make sure your current games are backed up, and help re-install Minecraft if there's a problem.

INTRODUCTION

Half of playing Minecraft is building—building shelters, bases, traps, and farms. Some people like building so much with Minecraft's blocks that that's pretty much all they do. Minecraft fans have built amazing things, joining up in teams to build intricate and massive structures like the space shuttle, fully detailed cities with hundreds of buildings, bridges, and parks, as well as epic scenes and buildings from *Lord of the Rings*, *Harry Potter*, and more. To see some of these, search online for "amazing Minecraft buildings."

For most people, though, building means a simple cube of cobblestone, with a couple panes of glass. Of course, if you're busy killing zombies and raising cows, building a snazzy home may be on the bottom of your list. You may find it more important to have a protective wall that a creeper can't explode.

However, if you have an architectural streak and you want to get started on building awesome homes and buildings in your Minecraft world, this book will show you the tricks the Minecraft experts use, including:

- How to build arches and spheres that look curved
- How to use depth and detail to make your buildings look realistic
- How to use steps, levers, trapdoors, and more for your furniture and amenities

To help you get started on some no-fail, amazing builds, this book includes step-by-step guides for building:

- An airship

- A fortified castle

- A pagoda

- A Mayan pyramid

- An underwater house

CHAPTER 1

GETTING STARTED

Building in Minecraft can be much more than making a shelter to keep you safe at night. If you like, you can spend time in Creative mode and take the time to build amazing things. In addition to homes, you can build almost anything you can find in the real world.

Blocks to Build With

You can basically build with any blocks, of course.

Traditional building materials. Traditional building materials are stone (including diorite, andesite, and granite) stone bricks, cobblestone, wood planks, and sandstone.

There are several variations on some of these blocks, such as mossy stone bricks, polished granite, and chiseled sandstone.

Traditional building materials that you can craft and find in Survival mode easily include stone, cobblestone, sandstone, bricks, glass, and their variations.

Wood logs. Wood logs from all six types of tree can be a great building material. You can place these on their sides to show the tree rings as well.

You can also use wood logs, upright or on their sides, for great effects and details.

Other blocks to use. Other building blocks that are a bit harder to get, but make great building materials, are stained clay, dyed wool, quartz, nether brick, and the blocks you find in ocean monuments—prismarine, dark prismarine, prismarine bricks, and sea lanterns. But you don't have to stick with traditional materials—you can use giant red mushroom blocks, dry sponges, anything you want at all. You probably want to avoid building with gravel and sand, as these can collapse. You should also avoid placing any flammable blocks within 4 blocks of a fire source, like lava. Flammable blocks can spread fire to other blocks and include wood, wooden items like fences, grass, vines, leaves, wool, hay, coal blocks, and bookshelves.

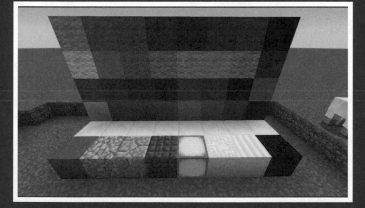

Dyed clay or wool, nether blocks, and the ocean monument blocks, can be more difficult to get or craft, but are terrific building materials.

Experiment with all of Minecraft's building blocks. You can re-purpose many for other uses. Two trapdoors can be the side arms for a chair and a redstone lever can be a sink faucet.

Basic Building Steps

The basic steps to follow when you build something are:

- Decide what you want to build. If you can, use photos or pictures as references or for inspiration.

- Decide how big it's going to be and how much space you need. Draw a simple blueprint or layout on paper.

- Find a location in your world for your build.

- Clear a flat area to start building.

- Create foundations for a building or markers that show where you are placing the front, back, and sides of your building.

- Build! Build the outer general structure first. (For homes and buildings, this would be the walls, floors, and roof.)

- Detail and decorate. Go over your structure, correcting mistakes, making improvements, and adding the details that will bring your creation to life.

Building to Scale

If you are recreating something from real life in Minecraft blocks, at "real-life" size within Minecraft, each Minecraft block is defined as 1 meter cubed, or 3.3 feet in each direction. So if you want to build your own house in Minecraft, you can measure the walls in feet or meters and know about how many Minecraft blocks it will take. You can't use half blocks in Minecraft, of course, only whole ones, so you will need to round up or down for the Minecraft measurement. For example, if my house is 45 feet wide by 30 feet deep, I'd divide by 3 to get the number of Minecraft blocks: 15 wide by 10 deep.

In Minecraft, 1 block is equivalent to 1 meter (or 3.3 feet) cubed in the real world. That means Steve is about 6 feet tall!

Building Giant Sizes

If you want to build a supersized version of something, find the real-world measurements and multiply them to get the final measurements. So if I wanted to build a giant skateboard, I would measure a real one in inches first—height, width, size of the wheels. This will give you the right proportions. Then you can build the skateboard in blocks instead of inches, or multiply all the measurements to make the design as large as you like.

Counting by Blocks

Many times in building something, you have to count the blocks you are using. You may need to make sure two walls are the same length or place two buildings the exact same size or distance from a third building. It's very easy to lose track of where you are when you're counting, or miss a block, or even get interrupted and forget. One way to keep track is to use some kind of marker every fifth block. That way, if you lose track, you can recount by fives to where you are.

Here are three ways to use counting markers: in a wall, place a different block every fifth block—you can go back to replace it later; punch a hole in the ground; or place a single block every five.

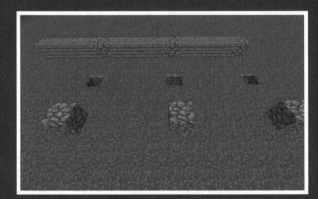

Building in Creative Mode

Building in Minecraft is much easier in Creative mode. In Creative mode, you have a never-ending supply of Minecraft blocks, so you don't need to plan on having the right materials. You can break blocks instantly with your hand. You can also fly around your building to place blocks, so you're in no danger of falling and damaging or killing yourself. And of course, mobs won't hurt you. With cheats on, you can change the time of day instantly so you can always work in daylight. You can also use the pick block key (usually the mouse's middle key) to select any block in your environment and put it in your hand, ready to place.

There are lots of advantages to building in Creative mode, like not being at risk of a long fall to the ground!

Building in Survival Mode

Although building in Creative mode is easier, building in Survival mode can be more satisfying. You have to do the work to locate, gather, and craft materials and plan efficiently so you don't waste these hard-won resources. You also feel pride when you have met the challenge of a time-consuming build accomplished in a hostile world.

So if you are up for the challenge of building in Survival mode, here are some tips:

- Build scaffolding from dirt blocks as you get higher. You can build dirt walkways and stairs outward from dirt beams to get to new places.

- Keep a stack of sand and a shovel so you can drop a pillar and shovel your way back down to the ground.

- If you are working really high above the ground, have a bucket of water (or a slime block) handy. For a long drop, you might just have enough time place water or slime on the ground before you hit it.

- Enchant your boots with feather falling to protect you from fall damage.

- Use the sneak key (Shift) with W and S so you can place blocks directly in front of you and underfoot.

In Survival mode, you can create a scaffold of dirt steps and beams to help you get to new heights.

In Survival, use the sneak key (Shift key) to creep over the edges of blocks. This allows you to place blocks in front of you at your feet and not fall to the ground. Hold the sneak key until you make it back to a solid block underfoot.

CHAPTER 2

MAKING CURVES AND ANGLES
WITH SQUARE BLOCKS

Round castle towers, glass survival domes, airship balloons, and arched bridges all are built with curves and angles. However, Minecraft blocks are famously lacking these curves—it's a square, ninety-degree world. To overcome this building obstacle, Minecraft players have learned to approximate curves and angles so well that, at a distance, you can build a Minecraft Golden Gate Bridge that looks like the real thing!

Here are some techniques and ideas that will get you building arches, angles, and circles like a pro.

Diagonals and Angles

A diagonal line isn't straight up and down, but it's not a curve either. It's a straight line that moves at an angle. The angle of a diagonal line may be steep or shallow, but it remains the same angle along the whole line. It rises a specific number of blocks for each block it travels horizontally.

From left to right: a slightly angled or shallow line, a steep diagonal, and a 45 degree angle.

To make a steep line, for each block that you place sideways, go up 2, 3, 4 or more blocks. It's the opposite for a shallow angle. For each block you rise, go 2, 3, 4 or more blocks along. Keep the ratio (1:3 or 3:1) the same the whole way along the line.

Placing Blocks Diagonally

Many times when you are building, especially when building curves, you need to place blocks diagonally to each other without having them actually touching sides.

For a diagonal block that is touching along one edge: Place the first block, one or two temporary blocks above it or to one side, and the final diagonal block where you want it. Then destroy the blocks in between. If you're working in Survival mode, you may want to use a "cheap" block like dirt as a temporary block.

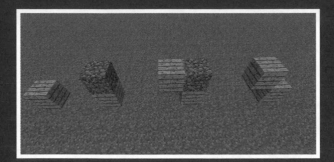

Use 1 temporary block to add a *diagonal* block along one edge, and then destroy the temporary block.

For a diagonal block that is touching just one corner: Do as above, but build out one more block from the top temporary block.

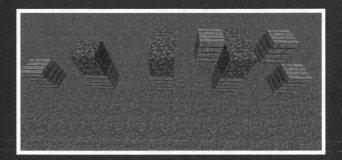

Use two temporary blocks to add a diagonal block that touches just one corner of another block, then destroy the two temporary blocks.

Curves

Whereas a diagonal or angled line keeps the same ratio of vertical to horizontal blocks as it goes, a curve changes the ratio. A curve can change slowly (a slight curve) or quickly (a steep curve).

To make a curve, you decrease the number of blocks that you place vertically (or horizontally) as you progress with almost every new step. (You can have a few steps that are angular, rather than curved, and still keep the overall curved look in Minecraft.)

The first curve is made from 1 step of 3 blocks at the bottom, 2 steps of 2 blocks, and 2 steps of 1 block. The second curve is made from 1 step of 4 blocks, 1 step of 3, 1 step of 2, and 3 steps of 1.

Circles

The easiest way to make a circle in Minecraft is to follow a pattern for a circle and exactly copy the number of blocks. You can find many patterns for circles, ellipses, and spheres online by searching for "Minecraft circle, sphere, ellipse patterns." But there are some simple techniques you can use to make your own circles by hand that look just as good.

First you decide how big a circle you want, in terms of its diameter. The diameter is the length of a straight line from one side of the circle to the other that passes through the circle's center point. Half of the diameter is the radius. It's the line from the circle center to the edge. It is easiest to create a circle with one center block, which means that the diameter will always be an odd number.

Next, create a cross whose two lines are the length of the diameter.

This cross is for a circle with a diameter of 15 blocks across.

At each end of the four spokes that come from the center, create four flat lines of the same length. The length of this line should be 5 blocks long for (odd) diameters of 9 to 17, 7 blocks long for diameters between 19 and 41, and 9 blocks long for diameters 43 to 49.

With a diameter of 15 blocks, spokes 5 blocks long are good. With the pink diameter block in the middle, you just add 2 blocks to either side for the total length of 5.

Once you've set the spokes, you'll need to make a curve in one corner of the circle. The curve needs to be symmetrical, so you can start by placing a line that is shorter than the spoke ends, starting from the spoke's end. Continue to shorten the additional lines until they meet at the center. You may need to experiment to make sure the quarter circle curve is symmetrical and looks good.

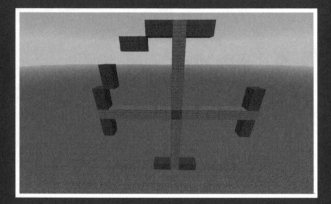

Start the curve by placing lines that are shorter than the length of the spoke ends. At the top, the line should be horizontal, and at the side, it should be vertical. For bigger circles, continue this way, decreasing the length of the lines till they meet in the middle. In this case, there is just one space left for a single block.

Once you've finished the quarter circle curve, copy it exactly to the other three parts of the circle.

Copy the curve pattern to the other three "corners" of the circle. If you don't want the center or the diameter in the finished circle, break those blocks.

You can use this basic technique to make circles of any size. Circles and arches can be replicated in Minecraft at small sizes, but they tend to look better and smoother the larger they are. A circle with a diameter of under 7 blocks tends to look more like a square.

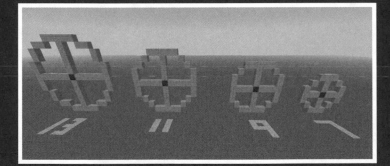

Here are patterns for four circles with diameters of 13, 11, 9, and 7 blocks.

Arches

You'll want to use arches for making amazing bridges, majestic entryways, and building details. You can make an arch with a half circle on top of two straight sides, but you can also make arches that are wide, shallow, or pointy. The one thing to keep in mind as you build an arch is to maintain the curve; each new line of blocks in the curve should be shorter or the same length as the previous. When the curve changes to point the other direction, each new line of blocks should be the same length or longer than the previous.

Notice that an arch is symmetrical and that the curve for each side of an arch goes from decreasing vertical lines to increasing horizontal lines (3, 3, 3, 2, 1, 1, 2, 3). You can make arches that are wider than this, narrower, higher, or steeper.

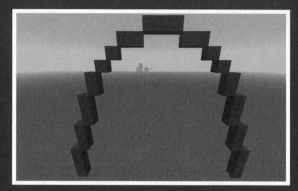

Spheres

Like circles, you can find patterns online that you can use to make spheres. You can make them yourself, although they are a bit harder than circles. In Minecraft, one way to make a sphere (or an ellipsoid) is by creating a series of circles placed one on top of the other. In the middle is the circle with the largest diameter, and as you move out from the middle, the circle diameter decreases, although the center has several circles of the same size. The tricky bit is that you don't decrease the size of the circle by a single block with each step. You need repeat circle sizes so that you create a curve as you decrease the circle size.

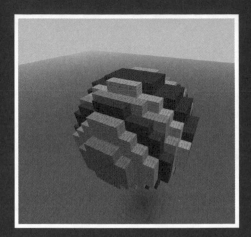

A sphere is essentially layers of smaller and smaller circles. When you make a sphere, you have to make sure that the slope created as the layered circles decrease in size (above, from the red circles to the smallest pink circle) is also a circle. This means that some circle layers will be repeated. In this sphere, the middle three red circle layers are identical.

To help you build a sphere, you can create an inner frame similar to the frame you created for a circle. This cross has a third bar showing the depth of the sphere. Then, around these three bars, you create identical circles. You can use these circles as a guide to the outside edges of the sphere as you fill in each layer of the sphere. It is easier to start with the horizontal middle and build up or down.

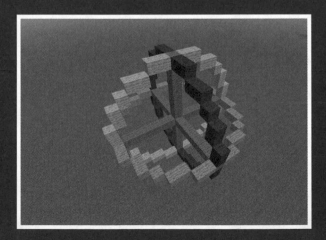

A frame for building a sphere. The central pink 3D cross shows the diameter of the sphere. Around this, you build three identical circles to show the curve of the outside of the sphere.

The sphere shape can be used for floating habitats, space ships, giant balls, and balloons. Often you will want to use just half a sphere shape to create domes for large towers, churches, mosques, and glass survival habitats.

Ellipses and Ellipsoids

Ellipses are flattened circles, and you can make them either by joining two arches together or using a central cross with one crosspiece shorter than the other. As with arches, you need to make sure each half is identical to the other. Ellipses can be used to help you make ellipsoids, which are elongated spheres. Ellipsoids can be used to make air ship balloons, sports stadiums, and more.

Use the same skills you use for making arches and circles to make ellipses.

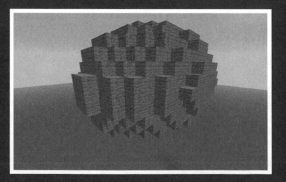

An ellipsoid is like an elongated sphere, and you can make it in the same way as a sphere. You can stack ever-decreasing circles on each other or create a frame of ellipses and a 3D cross.

CHAPTER 3
DESIGNING AND PLANNING YOUR HOME

F or building a simple, good-looking home in Survival mode that is beyond a basic cabin, but not a massive base or mansion, you can follow these steps.

1. Find your location.

Pick a relatively flat area for your home. You may want to be at the top of a hill for a view of your surroundings or by water, depending on how you like to play. Other things to keep in mind in selecting a location are:

(a) Clearing enough space for a defensive wall around your home.

(b) Clearing enough trees so that spiders and mobs can't jump over the wall or onto your roof.

(c) Deciding how much area you need around you for farming.

This location looks good for a simple house, with plenty of flat land good for farming and lots of animals.

2. Decide what rooms you need and how big they should be. At the minimum, you will need to place a bed, your chests, your crafting table, and your furnaces. You'll want room for your enchantment table, bookcases, and anvil. If you're into potions, you'll need room for the brewing station, a Nether wart farm, and some internal source of water. The one area that will probably expand the most is the area for your chests, as you collect and mine more and more stuff.

So the minimum rooms and sizes you will want are:

- **Bedroom:** a room at least 3×3

- **Crafting room:** to fit a crafting table, two 3-high stacks of double chests, and two stacks of two furnaces, make a 5×6 room at least, with 4-block high walls

- **Enchantment:** to fit fifteen bookshelves, the enchantment table, and an anvil, make a 5x5 room

- **Potion room:** to fit a 4×4 infinite water pool, a small Nether wart farm, several stacked chests, and the brewing stand, make a 6×7 room

 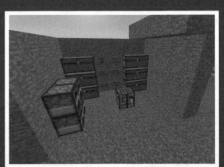

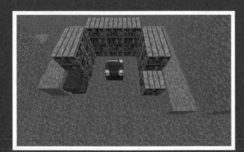 

You'll want your home to be big enough for your activities: spaces for sleeping, crafting, enchanting, and if you're ready, brewing.

If you want to merge rooms so that you use one large room for crafting and enchantment, add the minimum space you need for all your gear for both activities. If you want to make everything a little more spacious, add 1–3 blocks in each direction.

You may also want to add rooms just for decoration and hominess, such as an entry hall, a bathroom, a kitchen, and a living room.

Make a list of all the rooms you want and about how big they should be. You can use paper and pencil to make a rough layout, with the number of blocks you think each room and its walls will take up.

3. Clear your location to make it ready for building.

Add or destroy ground blocks to make an even surface. Clear trees and make sure you have enough space for your house and other needs. In general, for a smaller house, you will probably need an area that is at least 30x30 blocks.

Building on a Slope

Although building on flat land is easiest, you can also build on slope. Just start by choosing what level at which you want to build your bottom floor and construct a foundation out from there to include the rooms you need. Cut into the slope if necessary, and build walls down from the foundation to the slope.

If you want to build on a slope, build out what will be the bottom floor of your house for a foundation. You can fill in underneath the slope as you like—with a rocky base, wood frames, or more hillside.

4. Decide if you want your home to have a particular style.
Popular styles include traditional, cabin or country, modern, and medieval. Use the following types of base wall block for these styles. (If you don't want to stick to a particular style, select one of the main wall-building blocks to start with.)

- **Traditional:** red brick

- **Cabin/Country:** wood planks (any type)

- **Modern:** stone, snow, or plain quartz block

- **Medieval:** for plaster walls, use sandstone or snow; for a stone base, use cobblestone

5. Blueprint your home.
Make a blueprint for your home. If you like, you can do this first on paper, outside the game, to make it easier to fix and make changes. When you are ready to blueprint in Minecraft, place lines of stone blocks in the grass to show the walls of the house and between rooms. Also mark out with a different colored block where windows will go. Leave spaces for where doors or entrances will be.

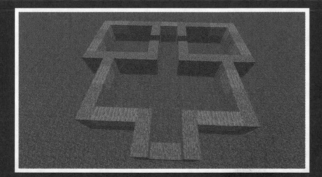

Here's a blueprint for a survival house using 2-block-high stone walls to show where the rooms are and blue wool to show where the windows will go. The entrance sticks out at the front, and there is a large room for crafting and chests. At the back will be a bedroom and a room for enchanting.

In general, the following layouts are typical for small homes in the following styles:

- **Traditional:** symmetrical or L-shaped
- **Cabin/Country:** square, rectangular, or L-shaped
- **Modern:** overlapping squares and rectangles (more than four corners!)
- **Medieval**: rectangular or L-shaped

Other things to take into account include:

- **Second floors and basements.** If you want to add additional floors or basements, now or later, make sure you have enough room for stairs, including landing space at the top and bottom. For a 4-block-high wall (where the ceiling/next floor is at the fifth block), and a staircase that is 2 blocks wide, you will need an area that is 7 blocks long and 2 blocks wide.

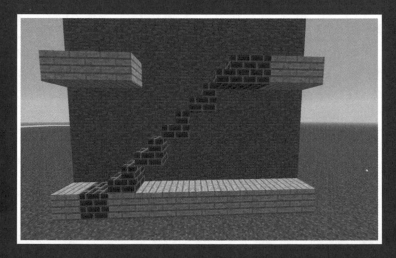

For simple 2-block-wide stairs, you'll need an area that is 7 blocks long and 2 blocks wide.

- **Front steps and porches.** If you want to add steps up to your entranceway or porches to the outside of your house, you will want to build a 2-block-high outline to show the walls and then fill in the interior with a choice of flooring, like wood planks. (If you want more than one level of steps up to your entryway, build your blueprint walls up to the height of the ground floor.)

- **Symmetry—odd or even.** If you want to place a single door or window in the center of a wall, you will need that wall to be an odd number of blocks long. If you want to place double doors in the center of a wall, the wall will need to be an even number of blocks long.

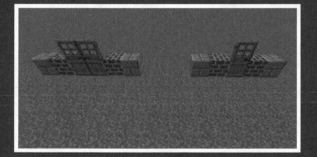

To center double doors along a wall, that wall will need to be an even number of blocks long. If you are centering a single door, the wall will need to be an odd number of blocks.

6. Review your blueprint.

Walk around your blueprint to see how you like it. Place some of your furniture in the outlined rooms to see where each piece will go. If you don't want to make and break furniture yet, use dirt blocks to show where things will fit. If you don't like something, redo your blueprint's mini walls until you are satisfied. Once you're happy, it's time to start building!

CHAPTER 4

BUILDING AND CUSTOMIZING YOUR SURVIVAL HOME

ow that you have created a blueprint for your home, decided the number of floors, and chosen the style (if any) you'd like to use, you can begin building! Once your basic build is done, you can add and remove parts and blocks for detailing and realism. But start with your walls, floors, and ceilings.

1. Build up all your walls.

For windows, leave spaces or fill them in with a temporary block, like dirt, so that you don't have to break and recreate glass panes. I've used blue wool here.

2. Dig out space for a basement.

If you want a basement, dig out at least 3 or 4 blocks deep. Place floor blocks. Replace the blocks underneath the blueprint walls with your basement wall blocks. Place a staircase to reach the ground floor or, when you fill out your ground floor in the next step, leave a hole for a ladder. Here, I've dug a massive basement to use for storage.

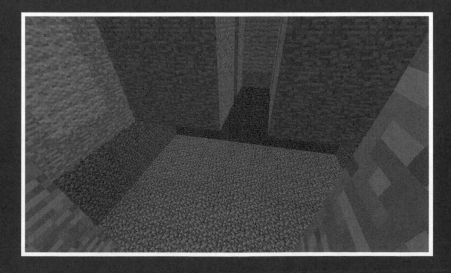

3. Fill out your floor.

Fill in your ground floor and add staircases or ladders to get to your basement, if you have one. Here, I've kept a hole for a ladder, and for the floor I've used the light birch wood and colored wool for carpet. Minecraft's carpet blocks are nice, but you can't put objects on top of carpet, so they are better used for open spaces where you won't place any furniture or objects like chests.

4. Build your upper stories.

If you have two or more stories, place the stairs up to this floor, fill out the floor, and place exterior walls for the second floor. Repeat for additional levels.

5. Add interior doors to rooms.

If you want doors to your rooms, add them. However, doors can be time-consuming to open and shut, and they require more building materials. You might want to have just having 1- or 2-block-wide entryways, if that works with your design.

6. Put a roof on your house.

There are many types of roof styles you can use. See chapter 7 for more roofing ideas. Here, I am building several low-pitched gabled roofs. Gabled roofs are sloped along two sides. Along the back section, the roof runs from left to right.

Atop the front section, the gable roof runs from front to back. I've adjusted it to have a flatter top. Over the entranceway, I've placed a hipped roof, sloping in at each exposed side. To create the shallow rise of all the roofs, I've used slabs of birch wood instead of full blocks. There was enough space to add clerestory windows (high windows, above eye-level) over the entranceway roof.

Check the inside of your roof. You may want to make sure your ceilings are flat and that walls meet the roof, especially if you've used slabs instead of full blocks. Here, because I want an open feeling, I've extended the stone walls as high as they can go to the roof and filled in any extra half spaces with birch slabs.

7. Finish the entranceway.

Here, I've added steps, extended a block from the door, added torches, and used stone blocks at each side of the steps. I've also found room above the door for some more clerestory windows.

8. Decorate the interior.

In a small survival house, there's often not enough space for large furniture pieces, and you need most of the space for chests, furnaces, and a crafting table. Here, I've added some chairs made of white quartz, with item frames for arms. I've also placed item frames on chests as labels. The frame items show what's inside each chest.

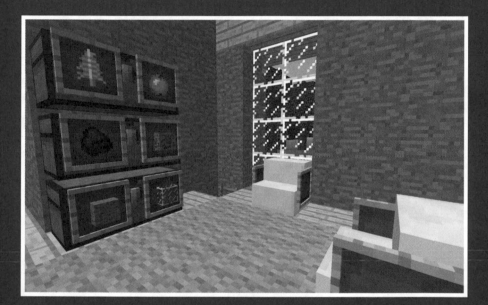

9. Add landscaping.

Your house or building can look pretty bare if you don't do some minimal landscaping. A great easy look is to add leaf blocks around the bottom of the house as edging. Here, I've added leaf blocks around the foundation of the house and two birch trees with torches to light them. The path is made of gravel and stone for a textured effect and edged with ferns. Two fence posts hold torches for extra light.

CHAPTER 5

SIX HOME DESIGNS

You've probably built a dozen survival cabins or square homes. But there are so many styles of architecture that you can easily switch it up if you feel like a change. Here are six home styles that work well for smaller homes. You can copy any of these for a unique look and feel for your home in Minecraft or take ideas from them.

Georgian House

This is a very traditional Georgian home. Georgian architecture refers to a style of building in England between 1620 and 1720 during the reigns of four kings all called George. Most Georgian family homes share the following characteristics:

- Red brick with white columns and detailing
- One or two stories high, and one or two rooms deep

- Strictly symmetrical, with the front door centered and windows placed symmetrically
- Two chimneys, one on each side
- Door capped with a small window (transom) or decorative cornice

The Georgian home above uses the following materials:

- **Walls:** red brick with white quartz for detailing
- **Columns:** pillar quartz blocks and quartz block stairs
- **Window details:** brick stairs beneath windows, snow blocks for shutters
- **Roof:** Nether brick stairs
- **Chimney:** brick blocks with flowerpots
- **Entranceway:** details

Hobbit House

Hobbits are imaginary creatures—short, humanlike characters from the stories by J.R.R. Tolkien and featured in the book and movie *The Hobbit*. They live in cozy, semi-underground homes built into hills and banks, with rounded doors and windows. Although rounded windows and doors on a small scale aren't possible in Minecraft, you can make a cozy, earthy home tunneled into a hill. The door and windows should be the only non-dirt features on the outside. You can shape the hill into a rounded shape to show off the rounded features of hobbit houses.

Modern House

Modern houses come in many styles, but in general they feature flat surfaces, large expanses of windows, and lighter colors. Minecraft's square blocks mean that it is especially easy to create a realistic modern building. This modern structure uses clay, stone, quartz, and glass. When you design a modern home, use different levels, corners, and insets to make the building interesting.

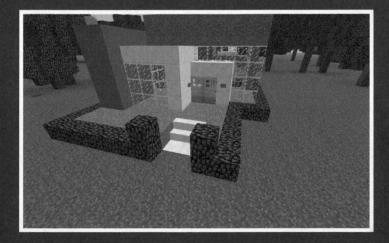

Earth Ship

Earth ships are earth-friendly homes built from natural and recycled materials, like tires filled with dirt and covered with plaster. They use passive solar power, which provides warmth by placing windows to catch the sun's rays. Many earth ships have curved, nature-like shapes and are built into a hillside. Mosaics are often used as a decoration because they can be built from broken tile and glass. Here, I've used emerald, lapis, and diamond ore for the mosaics and purple clay for the painted walls. A large, sloped, glass block window is placed to catch the sun.

Art Deco Home

Art deco is a decorative and architectural style popular in the 1920s, '30s, and '40s. Art deco buildings emphasize the vertical and have stylized geometrical, zigzag, or sunburst elements. They often utilize glass blocks for windows, stucco exterior walls painted in light, pastel colors, and flat roofs. Art deco homes frequently have curved windows or walls, but you can still build an art deco home in Minecraft using pink clay, quartz blocks, and glass blocks.

Pueblo Home

Pueblo homes are found in the American Southwest, particularly in Arizona and New Mexico. These feature stucco or adobe walls in earth tones, wood columns, and flat roofs. The roofs often have low walls, or parapets, edging them. Roof beams and inset metal rain gutters extend past the exterior wall at the roof level. Here, I've used hardened clay, with spruce wood, wood fencing, and wood buttons for the extruding rain gutters. A clay chimney has two flowerpots on it to create the extending pipes.

HOW TO DETAIL YOUR BUILDS

Most of us build our Minecraft homes simply. They are square or rectangular with straight, flat walls 3 or 4 blocks high and made completely out of brick or wood planks. To take your building to the next level and to make your homes both more exciting and realistic, follow the detailing principles that Minecraft building experts use.

Add Depth and Details

Add big or small insets, outsets or extrusions like pillars, and additional corners to your walls, whether they are perimeter walls or house walls. These create visual interest by breaking up the straight flat lines of a wall or a rectangular house. Here's an example of a wall with an extrusion (the wood pillars) and an inset (the chiseled stone blocks).

For example, you can add extra pillars to walls, use stair blocks to cap and base pillars, and add stone and wood buttons for extra details. When you are detailing, think about what elements you can add (or take away) at the top, bottom, and middles of walls—then experiment.

The basic process for adding details is to first construct your wall or building with its basic height and position.

Then look at what types of details you can add at the bottom, middle, and top of the wall. Add and remove blocks as you experiment and create. Here, I've replaced some of the top of the wall with fencing and added stairs at the bottom. The pattern is repeated the whole length of the wall.

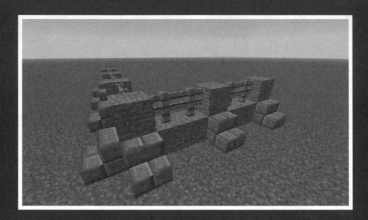

For more detailing, I've added torches to every other stone block column. To every stone block column, I've added stone buttons for extra depth.

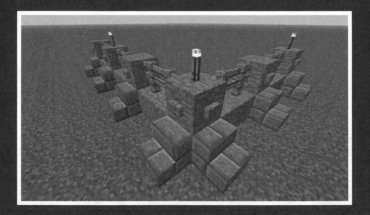

Blocks for Detailing

There are many blocks that Minecraft master builders use to detail their builds. When you are detailing, experiment with different colors, contrasting blocks, and patterns.

Common detailing blocks include: stairs, fences, leaves, slabs, ladders, buttons, iron bars, vines, glass panes, signs, item frames, flower pots, cobble and mossy cobble walls, and levers.

One caution: If you are using a redstone device for decoration, be careful not to place it somewhere it can be accidentally powered.

This wall uses stairs and slabs at the top, wood stairs at the bottom, and wood slabs in the insets. At the bottom of the insets are glowstone blocks, covered by leaf blocks.

The Right Door

Choose the right door for your build. A dark oak wood door works well with traditional homes, iron doors are great for industrial and modern buildings, while a jungle or birch wood door will look better with more casual or summery builds. The spruce wood door is perfect with fantasy or medieval buildings.

There are seven different doors you can use to match or contrast with your building's style and colors.

Use Patterns

When you add detailing, use different types of block in a pattern to break up the monotony of using the same brick. A few blocks have sides that are different; you can change which side is shown by the way you place the block.

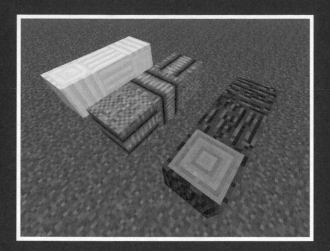

Pillared quartz, hay bales, and all the raw wood blocks have three types of sides you can use in making patterns.

Here, a wall made of sandstone uses the three types of sandstone, along with extruded pillars, roof wall, and sandstone stair detailing. The pattern of blocks and columns is repeated all the way along its length.

Use Random Patterns

Sometimes you don't need a strict, repeated pattern to create interest. You can break up a flat expanse of wall, floor, or roof by adding blocks in a random pattern. This means you can't see a real pattern repeated. This often works best if the blocks you are using have some similarity. For example, on an ancient stone building, like the castle shown later in this book, you can use stone brick and place random blocks of cracked stone brick and mossy stone brick.

This modern wall has a random pattern using soul sand, black clay, brown clay, and brown wool.

Add Contrast

Using two different blocks that contrast can really help your building stand out. You can add contrast with different colors (red and blue clay), texture (fluffy gray wool and smooth shiny quartz), and darkness (dark wood and light wood).

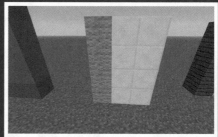

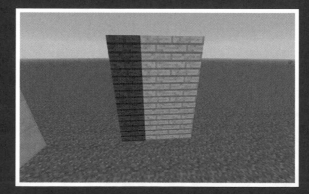

A common way to use contrast is to use a contrasting block to detail the corners of your buildings (almost as support pillars) and detailing around windows and doors. Here, a light birch wood is used for corners and detailing, and the main wall is made from the dark spruce wood block. Notice the different levels of depth by having the walls inset from the windows and pillars.

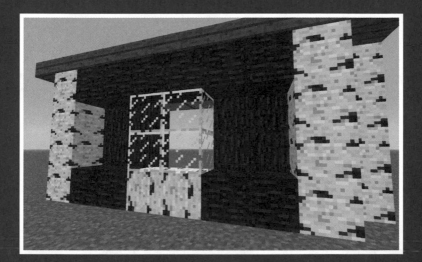

Use a Block Palette

If you have too many different blocks, colors, and textures in your build, it can look busy and unplanned. Master builders often create a block palette when they are planning. This is a set of at least three—and sometimes up to eight or so—blocks they will use for the build. The palette should include some blocks that complement each other and some that contrast or add texture. Notice how each has blocks that are similar color, with different texture, as well as some colors that are darker or different enough to provide contrast.

- Palette 1 (top): brick, pillar quartz block, quartz, chiseled quartz, red stained clay, nether quartz

- Palette 2 (middle): smooth sandstone, chiseled sandstone, sandstone, birch wood planks, pink stained clay, spruce wood planks

- Palette 3 (bottom): stone bricks, chiseled stone bricks, stone, spruce wood (raw), light gray wool, wool

CHAPTER 7

DETAILING WINDOWS, ROOFS, FLOORS, AND MORE

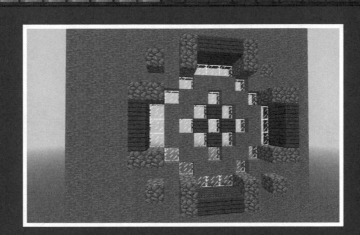

You can use the same basic principles we looked at in the last chapter to add detail and dimension to windows, stairs, paths and walkways, and roofs.

Windows

When you are detailing your building, look at ways your windows can add to the overall look. Some historic buildings work best with tall narrow windows, while modern buildings can look great with a large expanse of glass. Ways to add detail to windows include:

- Add stair blocks or other blocks above and below, or to the sides of the window.

- Inset or extrude the window from the wall.

- Add window boxes (make these out of dirt blocks surrounded by trapdoors).

- Instead of square windows, use arches, circles, crosses, or other shapes.

- Experiment with stained glass, glass blocks, and even fencing instead of glass.

Below are three windows showing what a difference detailing makes. At the right is a plain window using two glass blocks. The glass blocks make the surface of the wall totally flat.

In the middle window, you can see what a difference is made by just adding a stair block above and below and using glass panes. Glass panes add a level of depth to the flat wall.

And at the far left, the window area is entirely extruded by bringing the walls out. Extra stair blocks are added at the top for roofing, and leaf blocks bring in greenery, texture, and contrast.

Windows don't have to be square or use just glass. The diamond-like shape here is created using stair blocks. The nether fencing adds an extra layer of depth and contrast.

The arch of this window is extruded from the wall to add depth. It is made by placing stone brick stair blocks on whole stone brick blocks. The wall itself is detailed by placing cobble bricks randomly to give texture.

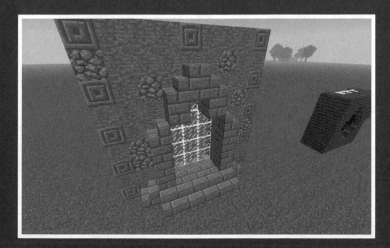

Paths and Walkways

Like walls, you can improve straight, single-block paths by adding patterns and depth. You can use the same types of blocks you use to detail walls. Elements to add to paths include:

- Use slabs and different levels and materials for path borders and walls.

- Raise the walkway height from the ground around it, or create a pattern by using half-slabs in place of some full blocks.

- Add arches or other coverings.

This pathway is raised and uses raw wood pillars at different heights, joined by fencing to create visual interest and depth. The wood blocks placed evenly along the walkway also visually break up the flat expanse of wood.

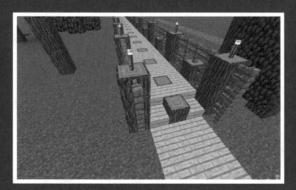

Depth and pattern in this stone brick walkway is added by using half-slabs at regular intervals along the pathway and stairs along the edges. Contrast is added by using stone brick, cobble, and chiseled brick.

Walkways don't have to be formal or use repeating patterns. Here's a stone pathway curving through the forest. I've placed cobblestone, mossy cobble, stone, and gray wool randomly to make the path look old and run-down. To light the path, I've embedded single glowstone blocks in the ground and covered them with bushes made of leaf blocks.

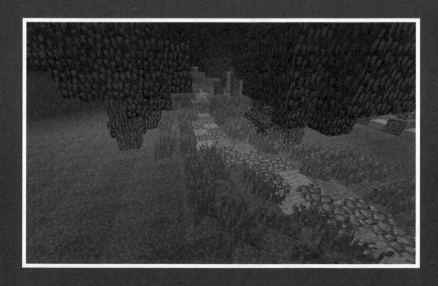

Stairs

The typical stair is a set of stair blocks using all the same material. But you don't have to stick to this. You can add landings and use slabs instead of stairs for a shallower slope. You can also use spiral stairs. Spiral stairs save space, although they make it more difficult to go up and down.

There are many ways to make spiral stairs. You can use stair blocks with slabs for landings or slabs alone. The stairs on the left are made from stair blocks and slabs, and the middle and right-hand stairs use slabs only. The stairs on the right also don't curve around a central column-like space; they simply run back and forth side-by-side.

As you can see, you can attach the step blocks around a central column or let them float. Single block-wide spiral stairs take up the least amount of room but are the most difficult to climb up. If you don't have an enclosing wall for them, you can fall off them more easily.

Double-wide spiral stairs are much easier to climb. The stairs on the left curve around a 4-block-wide column and the ones on the right curve around a single-block column.

Plan your steps out so that you have 3 blocks of space above each step to allow you through!

Detail stairs by using different blocks for handrails or walls around the stairs. With 3-block-wide or wider stairs, you can also include different stair blocks for the steps. This stone brick stair is 3 blocks wide, so I've used wood stairs in the middle for contrast. I've used ladders on the outside as decoration. The stair walls are made from stone brick topped by fencing.

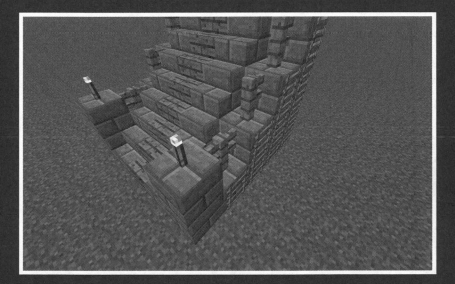

This simple wood stair uses slabs instead of stair blocks, which makes a less steep slope. I've used fencing for the handrail, and every other step has green carpet covering to add contrast.

Floors

Experiment with all types of blocks for flooring. As with walls and walkways, you can repeat patterns with contrasting blocks, use a random pattern of similar blocks, and make patterns with the floor's height by using half-slabs.

If you have a large space to use up, you can make a large pattern, like this one below. It is a little like a parquet wood floor and uses four different wood planks.

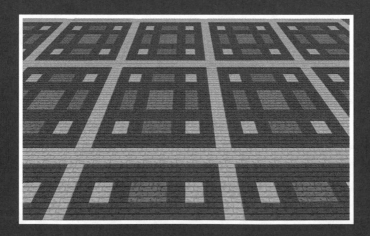

This floor uses different levels for depth and different stone blocks to add texture and pattern. The central square is made by placing steps around each other and adding a full height block in the center. Slabs are used for the cross pattern.

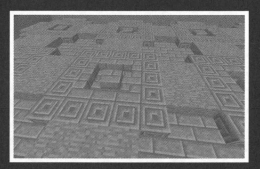

Roofs

Just as with walls, windows, floors, and stairs, you can use different blocks, textures, and colors to detail your roofs. First of all, you don't have to stick to using either a flat roof or the traditional gabled roof that slopes up along two sides to meet at the apex in the center. Other types of roofs are hipped roofs, shed roofs, saltbox roofs, and gambrel roofs.

A gabled roof slopes on two sides.

A hipped roof slopes on all sides, like a pyramid.

A shed roof slopes on just one side and is usually found on small buildings like sheds or extensions to a house.

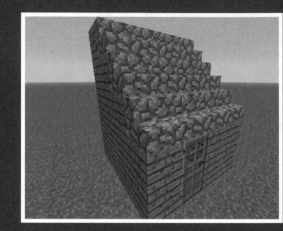

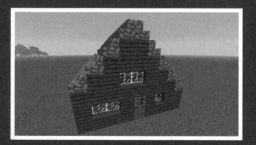

A saltbox roof slopes to a lower level on one side than the other. It's most commonly found on farmhouses.

A gambrel roof has a shallower pitch or slope at the top and a steeper pitch on the sides.

Other roofing techniques:

- Make the roofs steeper by using steep pitches (slopes).

- Make roofs shallower by using shallow pitches and slabs.

- Curve the roof by using the same types of slopes you use in circles and arches.

- Combine two types of roof. For example, you can combine a shed roof with a gabled roof.

Use the techniques you've learned with circles and arches to make curved roofs.

Centering Roofs

If you are using a sloped roof, take a look at how many blocks wide your building is. If it is an odd number of blocks wide, the top of your roof will be a single block, as on the left below. You won't be able to put a stair block at the top, but you can place a slab. If your building is an even number of blocks wide, you will have 2 blocks at the top and be able to place two stair blocks against each other.

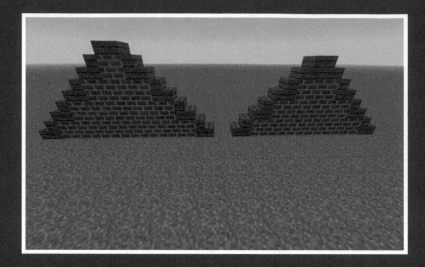

Detailing Roofs

For detailing roofs, you can use different types of stair blocks or slabs at different levels. You can add dormers and chimneys, as in the picture below. You can add depth by extending the roof out from the building.

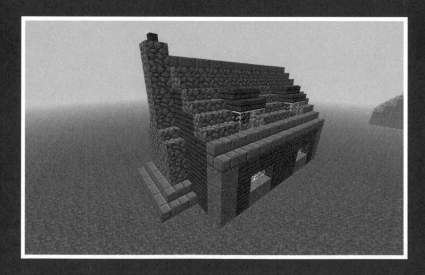

A flat roof can be detailed with different blocks and levels. This one uses chiseled stone, wood planks, cobblestone, stone, and stone slabs.

However, if your building is heavily detailed, it may be better to keep your roof fairly simple, so that it doesn't compete visually with the creativity of the walls.

CHAPTER 8

GLASS DOME

You can build a Minecraft biosphere in a desert with a glass dome—or, even better, with a series of glass domes connected by corridors. Because glass lets sunlight through, your farms will grow just as well inside a dome. If you keep the dome fully lit, you can also be completely protected from mobs. You can build your dome in any biome, but it's probably most impressive in a desert, mesa, or underwater.

Building a dome is the same thing as building a half sphere. You place increasingly smaller circles, one or more blocks deep, on top of each other. Follow the steps below to build a sphere that is 28 blocks in diameter. In these steps, I've used different colored blocks to help you see where to position the blocks, but you can build all the circles with glass blocks. If you have difficulty keeping track of the positions, you can build each new circle in a different color of block. Then, at the end, you can replace each block with a glass block.

One thing that can help in building circles and spheres is to concentrate on getting just one quarter of the circle right. Once that is done, you can copy the pattern to the other quarters of the circle.

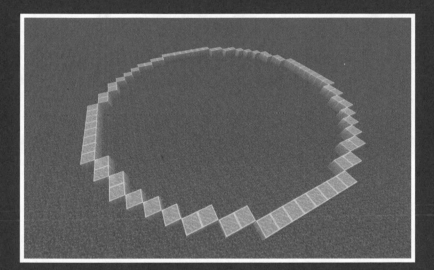

1. Build the first circle.

The first circle has "ends," or long sides, that are 8 blocks long. Each of the four curves begins and ends a set of 2 blocks connected by 3 single blocks in the center. Because the diameter of the dome is 28 blocks, the total height should be 14 blocks. However, to give some extra height, and to easily fit a door, we are adding an extra bottom circle.

2. Build the second and third circles.

Raise the first circle an additional 2 blocks for a total of 3 blocks of height.

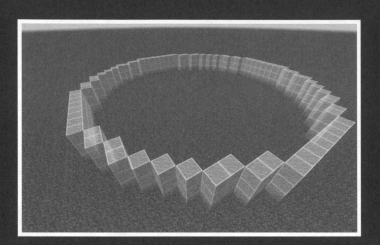

3. Build the fourth circle.

The fourth circle is very similar to the first three, but the long sides are only 6 blocks long, and the first set of blocks of the curve are 3 blocks long.

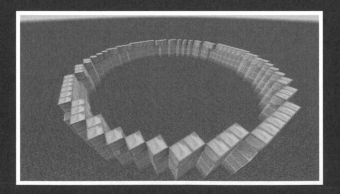

4. Build the fifth circle.

The fifth circle has ends or sides that are only 4 blocks long.

5. Build the sixth circle.

The sixth circle is the first one that is smaller in width (at the long ends) than the circles beneath. Notice how the long ends are 8 blocks long, and many of the blocks don't rest on a block beneath them.

6. Build the seventh circle.
The seventh circle has long ends that are 6 blocks long.

7. Build the eighth circle.
The eighth circle is a block smaller or inside the circle beneath, with long ends that are 10 blocks long.

8. Build the ninth circle.

The ninth circle has long ends that are 6 blocks long.

9. Build the tenth circle.

This circle is also smaller than the ninth, with 8-block-long ends.

10. Build the eleventh circle.
The eleventh circle is also smaller than the previous, with 8-block-long ends.

11. Build the twelfth circle.
The twelfth circle is smaller than the previous, again with 8-block-long ends.

12. Build the thirteenth circle.
The thirteenth circle has multiple blocks to create a flatter curve.

13. Build the fourteenth circle.
The fourteenth circle doesn't rest on any of the blocks of the circle below it.

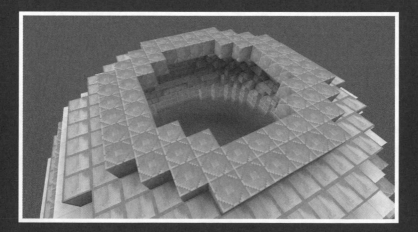

14. Finish the final circle.
The final circle is filled in. Like the previous circle, it doesn't rest on any of the blocks below.

15. Complete the dome.
If you have been using differently colored blocks to keep track of your circles, now is the time to replace all of the blocks with glass blocks. Add one or more doors and customize the interior as a house, garden, jungle, or animal pen. This dome below is customized as a jungle retreat and ocelot sanctuary. There are jungle trees, ferns, vines, bushes made of leaf blocks, a path, a bench, and, of course, ocelots!

CHAPTER 9

UNDERWATER HOME

What could be cooler than an underwater base? On top of being pretty impressive, an underwater home gives you more protection from mobs and explosions than land-based homes. You can be sure a creeper isn't sneaking around outside! On the other hand, building underwater is harder than above ground, especially in Survival mode. Once your underwater home is built, you also have to be careful not to accidentally break an exterior wall block and flood your home. (If you do break a block, you can usually fill it pretty quickly with any other block for a temporary stopgap.)

There are a couple of good techniques for building an under-water home. In one, you build up walls from the ocean bottom, and in the other, you drop a sand mold onto the ocean floor. The first works better for shallower depths.

Underwater Building in Survival Mode

If you are building in Survival mode, there are several ways to help you breathe underwater.

- **Create air bubbles with blocks.** Several block types (fences, signs, doors, glass panes, iron bars, trapdoors, ladders) create an air bubble next to them. If you place these and stand next to them, you can breathe and replenish your air. If you are building very deep, you can create a pillar of sand and attach ladders to it. You can also place a torch to create a temporary air pocket, although the torch will immediately drop.

- **Emergency breathe with a bucket.** You can click an empty bucket in front of you. To reuse, click the bucket again to empty it.

- **Enchantments and potions.** Use a helmet with Respiration or Aqua Affinity or a Potion of Water Breathing.

Lighting the Depths

It can be very dark underwater, which makes it difficult to build. You can place glowstone blocks, sea lanterns, and jack o' lanterns to add light or use a Potion of Night Vision. You can also create a small "hut" of fences to enclose a torch on at least two sides and above. (The torch has to be placed last.)

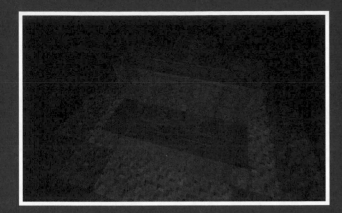

Torches need air to stay alight, so you can use fences to surround a torch.

Method 1: Walls to Surface Mold

In this underwater building method, you create a blueprint or layout in dirt, above water, to show where your exterior walls will go. You can include walls that will form a tunnel from the land to your house.

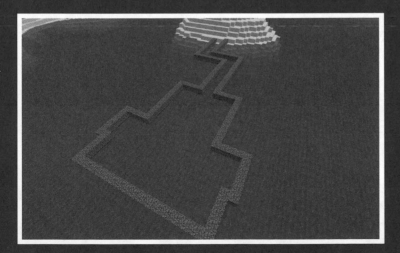

Here is a blueprint for the exterior walls of an underwater home, built on the ocean surface. The walls extend to the land, to help in building an underwater tunnel to the home.

You then build these walls down to the level where you want your floor to be. Use dirt blocks as you go down until you reach the ceiling. For example, if you want to have your ceiling 5 or so blocks below the surface, start with 5 dirt blocks. Then use the block you want for the ceiling. Then place wall or window blocks as far as your floor, and then the floor block. The floor block doesn't need to be on the ocean floor.

Here, you can see the walls built down, first with dirt to reach the ceiling level. Then glass blocks are used here for the walls and finally stone for the floor.

You then build in your floor, so you've essentially created a large tub, filled with water.

The floor is built in here with stone and glass to see through, because the floor is not on the sea floor.

If you don't want your home to look like it is floating, you can build pillars down to the ocean floor.

Back on the surface, drop sand or gravel blocks to fill up the interior of your house, all the way to the ocean surface. This clears the water from your home.

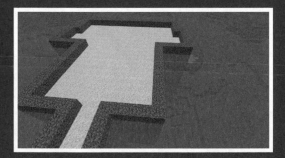

Here the interior is filled with sand. This removes air from the interior, and when you destroy the sand, the interior will be cleared of water.

Next, you break the sand or gravel, leaving air in its place. To quickly get rid of the sand, first dig down to the floor. Then break a floor-level sand block next to you and quickly fill the floor of that space with a torch. The torch will burn the sand falling above it.

Once the sand is removed, fill in the ceiling layer, including the ceiling of the entrance tunnel, if you have one. Back at land, make sure to build up steps to the surface.

This tunnel entrance has been enclosed with sandstone and a door.

Filling in the ceiling, 4 blocks below surface level. Glass blocks will allow a little more light from the surface to get in.

Finally, you can break the temporary dirt walls, letting the water flow in above the house. Now you can enter your house from your tunnel and make any final changes. It is pretty easy to break a block and quickly fill it with another if you decide you want to change the look or you see a mistake.

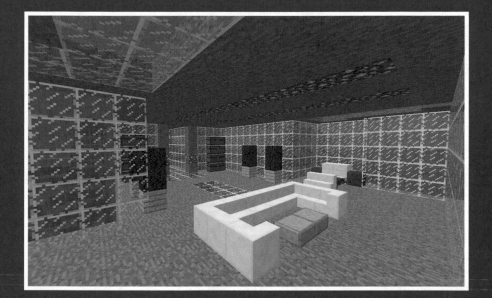

The finished underwater house, with glowstone blocks used for lighting.

Method 2: Mold on a Platform

In this technique, first level the sea floor where you are placing the home. Above the water, build a temporary platform that is the width and length of your home. One way to start building right over the ocean, without a beam extending from the land, is to first place a lily pad block on the water.

You can place a lily pad on water and a block above that to start building.

Then you can place a dirt block over the lily pad as the start of your platform.

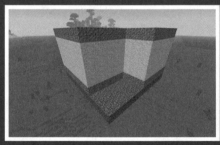

Build a mold of your home in sand or gravel on a platform. Here, the gravel shows what will eventually be the floor and roof.

When your platform is finished, build the shape of your home in gravel or sand. Make sure the home shape is all filled in. When you are satisfied, destroy the platform blocks so that the columns of sand or gravel drop down in place to land in position on the ocean floor.

 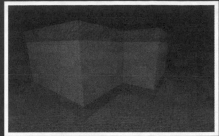

The sand or gravel mold will drop to the ocean
floor when you destroy the platform it's on.

When you destroy the dirt platform, the sand and gravel mold
drops to the sea floor. Then you need to swim underwater and
place the exterior wall and roof blocks over the mold.

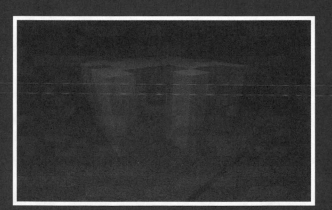

Here is the mold covered
with walls and ceilings
of sandstone and glass
blocks for windows. The
windows extend onto
the ceiling as well for an
overhead view.

You can use glass blocks for windows. Once the mold is sealed
over, break in on one wall. Use a ladder to make an air space
on the inside of the broken wall.

Place ladder blocks when you break into your house to create an air space and prevent water from flooding in.

Then you can start destroying the sand or gravel blocks inside your walls and roof. Once that is done, fill in your floor.

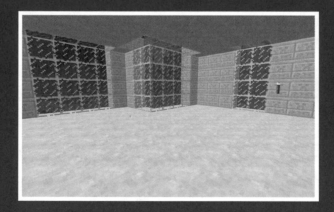

The finished home with floor filled in.

One way to make an exit is to place solid blocks, with ladder blocks attached, all the way to the ocean surface. At the top, you can make a landing with a dock or cove for a boat.

Here is a landing spot for the ladder entrance, with a sand cove (built on a dirt foundation) to hold a boat. You can use dirt blocks to seal off the cove to keep your boat safe.

CHAPTER 10

JAPANESE PAGODA

A pagoda is a building that has many stories and wide eaves that are often curved at the tips. Pagodas have been built in China, Japan, India, Vietnam, and other East Asian countries. They traditionally have been used for religious worship.

1. Build a raised foundation.
Build a raised foundation of stone or cobble that is 16x16 blocks square. Add steps in the center of one of the sides.

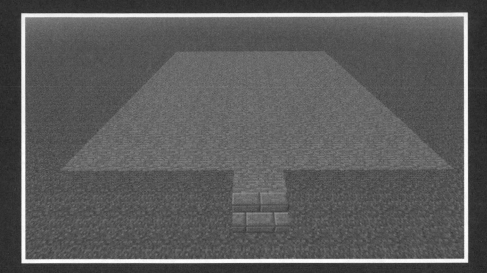

2. Build the first floor.

The building will be 10x10 blocks, with a 2-block entrance in the center of each of the four walls. Build the first floor in the center of the foundation. The floor is 4 blocks high. Use snow for the walls and red wool for the corner columns. Fill the top two rows in each entrance with one row of snow and a row of black wool.

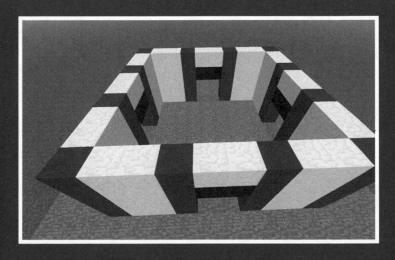

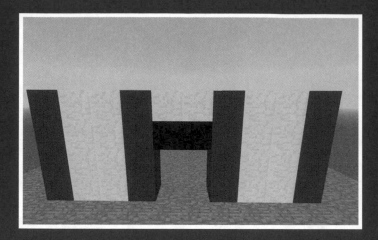

3. Add a cobblestone layer.
Top the first floor with a 1-block layer of cobblestone.

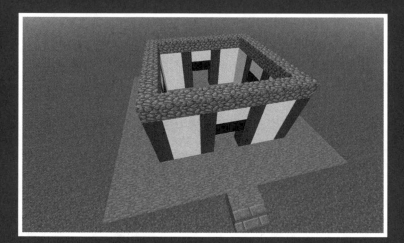

4. Build three more stories.
Build three more identical floors, using the first floor as your guide. Top each floor with a layer of cobblestone.

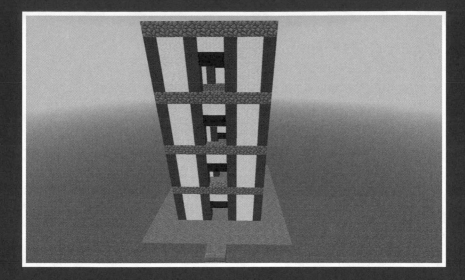

5. Add three roofs.
At each of the first three cobblestone layers of the building, build out a roof made of three levels of Nether brick slabs. Use a wood slab if you don't have access to Nether brick.

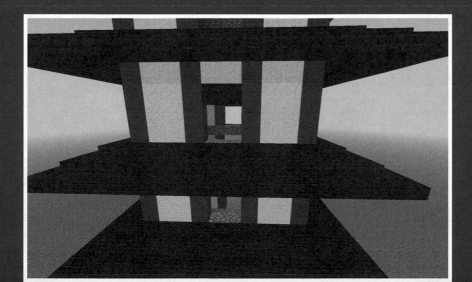

6. Add raised corners to the roofs.

Each roof is made of three levels of slabs. To build the raised corners of the pagoda roofs, first locate the outermost corner of the middle slab level. In this picture, this slab is the sandstone slab, just to show it clearly. From the level of slabs below this, remove the three slabs around it.

Next, add two slabs to the exposed sides of the corner slab. Use the same type of slab as the rest of the roof.

Lastly, add a slab in the empty corner, one slab level up as shown. (The slab is cobblestone in the picture to help show its position, but you should use the same roof slab as you've used elsewhere.)

Repeat these steps for each corner of each roof.

7. Add entrance details.

At the pagoda entrance, add fence posts rising up and connecting to the roof with another slab. Fence in toward the entranceway and around the building. Add torches to the corners.

8. Add fence detailing on top of roofs.

On top of each roof and right next to the wall, place fence around the building.

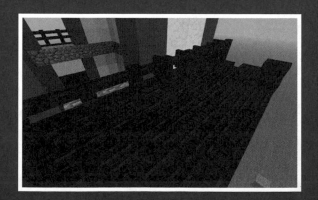

9. Add fence detailing below each roof.

Beneath the roof, place fence all the way around the building. Attach the fencing to the second slab in. Add torches for light to the corners.

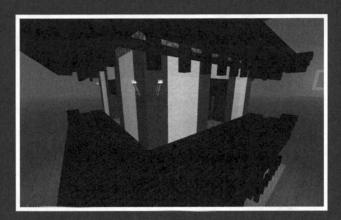

10. Begin building the top roof.

For the top roof, first build out from the cobblestone layer as you did with the three middle roofs, using three levels of slab. Add the same raised corners to the top roof as you did with the middle roofs.

11. Finish the top roof.

Next build inward. From the cobblestone base inward, use slabs for three levels, then use a slab topped with a stair block. The final level should be a solid block. Repeat this pattern on each side of the pagoda.

The final roof should look like this.

12. Customize your pagoda.

Inside your pagoda, you can add floors and decorate if you like. For a Japanese feel, surround your pagoda with a garden of birch trees, ponds and lily pads, wood walkways, and bridges. Here, the interior is decorated with lily pads in item frames, dead bushes in flower vases, and torches on Nether brick fence. You can make a traditional reed, or tatami mat, from hay bales. (You can use different faces of the hay bale block depending on how you click to place the bale.) In the center of the tatami mat is a special area (made of black wool) for a Japanese tea ceremony.

CHAPTER II

FORTIFIED CASTLE

A fortified castle is a castle that has additional defensive features, such as a perimeter wall. Follow these steps to build an impressive castle with a barbican, or gated entrance building, and a defensive wall. You can adjust the measurements given to make the castle, towers, or walls bigger. The most important measurement is aligning the towers with each other so that connecting walls between them will run straight from one tower to the next.

1. Build four castle towers.

Each tower is 5x5 blocks square and 20 blocks high. The towers should form a square, with each tower 10 blocks from the next. Use colored wool to help you measure. As you build the castle, use a mix of stone bricks, cracked stone bricks, and mossy stone bricks. This will give the castle a timeworn appearance.

2. Build up the castle's walls.

Use the pattern below to build up the castle walls to 14 blocks high. The longest section of the wall is 5 blocks wide and has 2-block-wide sections at either side. The 2-block sections should be center aligned to the tower wall.

Select which of the four walls will be the front, and create an entranceway that is 4 blocks high and 3 blocks wide.

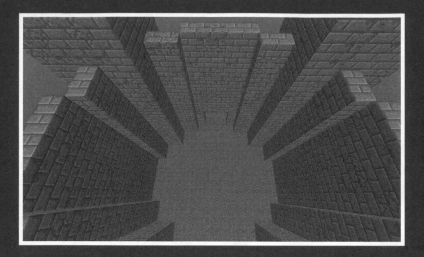

3. Plan the defensive wall.

The defensive perimeter of the castle will be four towers, connected by high walls with walkways. Use colored blocks to measure the center of each of the four towers, where the four towers will go, and to make sure they will line up with each other. Here, the corners where the center of the towers will be placed will be 18 blocks away from the front of the castle, 10 blocks from the sides, and 13 from the back.

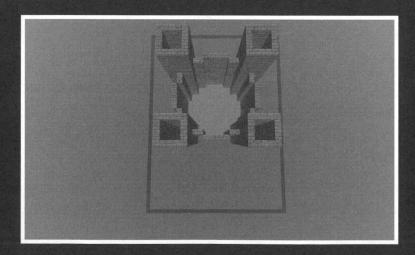

4. Build the outer towers.

Create the four outer towers, one at each corner, using the pattern below. The longest sides are 3 blocks wide. The center of the tower should be the same block as the red wool outline. Raise the towers 11 blocks high.

5. Roof each outer tower.

Roof each tower with a 7×7 platform. Add additional walls one block high, and one block out, on each side as shown.

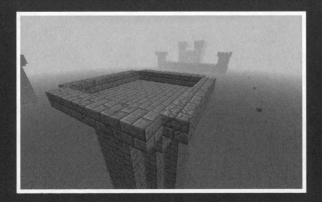

6. Add detailing to the tower.
Add upside-down stair blocks beneath the tower platforms.

7. Build the barbican.
The barbican will provide entrance to the castle grounds. Build the barbican 11 blocks wide, 7 blocks high, and 6 blocks deep. It should be aligned with the two front towers and center aligned with the castle's entranceway.

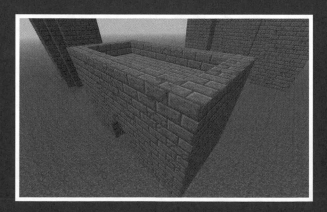

8. Create the barbican's entranceway.

Create an arched entry-way to the barbican as shown. It is 3 blocks wide and 3 blocks high, with upside-down stairs placed to create the arch.

9. Build the second circular section.

Add defensive walls between all four of the external towers and the barbican. The wall is made of two 5-block-high walls spaced 3 blocks apart. An upper walkway connects the two walls as shown.

10. Finish the castle towers.

On the outside of the four castle towers, add additional 5-block-wide by 4-block-high panels on each side at the top. These will meet diagonally at each side. These panels should extend higher than the inner wall by 1 block.

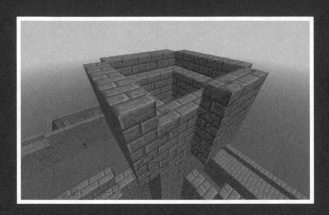

11. Finish the castle.

Add a roof to the castle, one block below the outer wall. Customize the interior as you like by adding floors, rooms, and halls.

12. Add crenellations.

Add crenellations by placing single blocks, spaced a block apart, to the tops of the castle towers, perimeter walls, and barbican.

13. Add windows.

Add evenly spaced, tall windows to the castle and the barbican, using iron bars to fill them in.

14. Add cobblestone paths.
Add a cobblestone path from the barbican to and around the castle. Add torches outside the castle entranceway and short columns with torches for the cobblestone path. Add iron bars around the inside frame of the castle door as a portcullis.

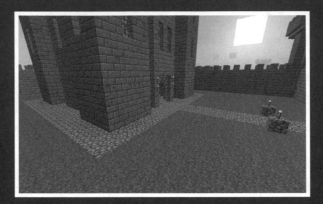

15. Add detailing to the barbican entrance.
Add iron bars for a portcullis at the inner and outer entrances of the barbican. Add columns with torches outside the outer entrance.

16. Customize the castle.
You'll now want to go through the castle, defensive walls and towers, and barbican to add rooms, floors, ceilings, staircases, ladders, and any more windows you want. This castle is customized with a moat and bridge just outside the perimeter wall.

CHAPTER 12

AIR SHIP

Air ships were the first form of controlled and powered air transportation and were very popular in the early 1900s. Although there are quite a few types of air ship, they all use a large bag filled with a gas that is lighter than air to fly. The bag is typically elongated, like the ellipsoids described in chapter 2, and a passenger cabin is attached to the bottom of the gas bag. Follow these steps to build your own air ship.

1. Build the first frame.
Build the central frame for the balloon. First, use dirt to build a column at least 25 blocks high that will mark the bottom center of the balloon. Then build a cross as a frame for the center of

the balloon. This frame will be used to build a circle later. Each of the four arms of the cross should be 6 blocks long. Use a different colored block to mark the circle's center. Here, I've used wood planks.

2. Build the second frame.

Build the center of the circle out horizontally with 10 blocks. I've used different wood planks to help in counting. Use the tenth block as the center to build the frame for a circle with four arms that are each 5 blocks long. I've used different colored wool for each crossed frame, to help distinguish each one, but you can use any blocks you like.

3. Build the third frame.

Build the central beam out another 3 blocks. Using the third block as a center, create a crossed frame with arms 4 blocks long.

4. Build the fourth frame.

Build the central beam out another 3 blocks. With the third block as the center, build a crossed frame with arms 3 blocks long.

5. Build the fifth frame.
Build the central beam out another 2 blocks. On the last block, build a frame with arms 2 blocks long.

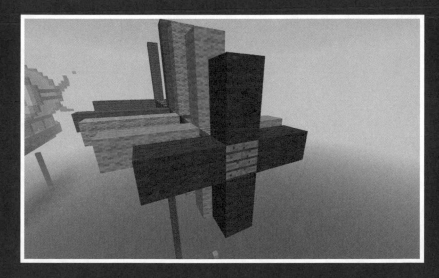

6. Build the sixth frame.

The sixth frame is right next to the fifth frame, with arms that are 1 block long.

7. Finish the framing.

Repeat steps 3 through 7 to build the frames for the other side of the balloon. The final balloon skeleton should look like the picture below. You can now use these frames to create circles, duplicating the circles in the same way as when you make a sphere. You can use this same process—building a series of frames for circles—for building ovoids of any size.

8. Build the first circle.

Build the first circle around the central frame as shown. The long sides of the circle, at the end of each arm, are 5 blocks long. Here, I am using colored wool to match the frame, but you can use white wool or any wool color you want for the finished balloon. The black wool blocks show where the circle touches at the end of the four frame arms.

9. Build out the central circular section.

Extend this central circle on both sides 9 blocks out to the second frame on either side.

10. Build the second circular section.

On the second frame on each side, build a circle as shown and make it 3 blocks deep. The long side, at the end of each arm, is 5 blocks long.

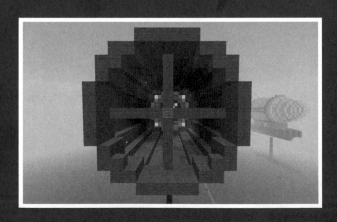

11. Build the third circular section.
Build the third frame's circle as shown and make it 3 blocks deep.

12. Build the fourth circular section.
Build the fourth frame's circle and make it 2 blocks deep. The long ends are 5 blocks long.

13. Build the fifth circle.
Build the fifth frame's circle as shown. The long ends are also 5 blocks long.

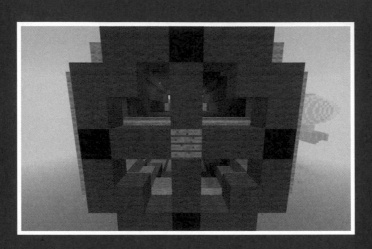

14. Build the sixth circle.
Build the sixth frame's circle. The long ends here are 3 blocks long.

15. Fill in any gaps.
You may see that there are some holes in the surface. Fill these in so there are no gaps leading to the interior.

If you have used white wool for the balloon, it will look like the following figure.

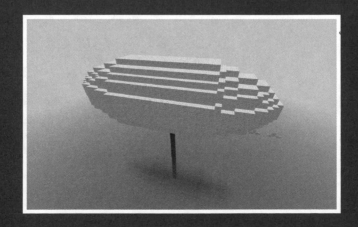

16. Add a frame to the balloon.

Now use wood blocks to create a frame around the balloon that will support the passenger cabin. The two screenshots show the side and the bottom of the frame.

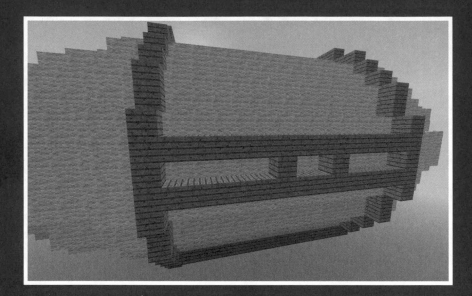

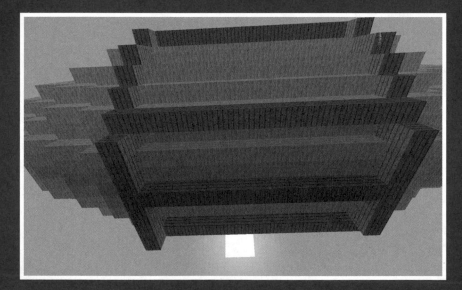

17. Add hanging supports.

Add 3-block-high columns at the four bottom corners of the balloon's wooden frame. The passenger "ship" will hang from these.

18. Shape the bottom of the ship.

On one end, build the outer shape of the ship.

19. Build out the ship bottom.

Extend this ship to the two columns on the other end.

20. Create the curve for the ship's ends.

Build the curve for the end of the ship.

21. Build in the ship's end.
Complete the ship's end by filling in the blocks, curving toward the tip of the ship.

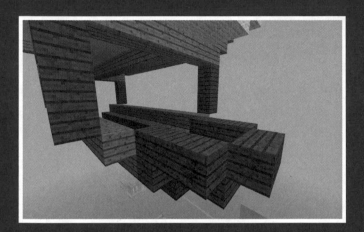

22. Build the other end of the ship.
Repeat this on the other end of the ship so that both ends of the ship are closed in.

23. Add a frame for a propeller.

First add a supporting frame made of wood blocks around one side of the ship as shown. Add a 2-block extension for attaching the propeller.

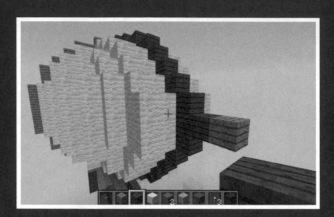

24. Build the base of the propeller.

Build out the propeller shape, 1 block deep in a dark wood plank.

25. Add detailing to the propeller.
On top of the base propeller shape, build the inner propeller shape, one block deep, in a lighter wood. Use dark wood for the center, and place a wood button in the center.

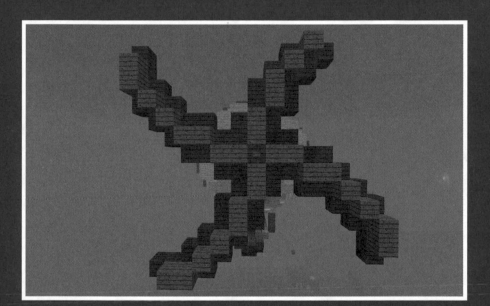

26. Customize your air ship.
Finalize your ship by adding detailing, modifying the ship's shape, and installing lighting. Here, I've enclosed the center part of the ship and added a roof, windows, and doors. I added stair blocks for detailing and used fence posts for the ship's tether to the ground.

INTRODUCTION

If you are new to the game, fighting the mobs in Minecraft can be a bit scary. But once you get used to the mobs and fighting them (and get used to occasionally dying!), it can be a lot of fun. I was not much of a fighter at first, but now I stay up at night (Minecraft night) just to find and kill some skellies, zombies, and Creepers. It's also a great way to get more experience points so you can enchant more weapons, armor, and tools.

This book has all the information you need to improve your fighting skills against the different mobs in Minecraft, from Blazes to zombie pigmen, and some tips to help you in PvP, as well. You'll learn more about your weapons, and how to enchant them and use potions. The mob profile pages examine each neutral and hostile mob: where you'll find it, how to kill it, and what experience points and drops it will give you. On each page you'll also find the number of strikes needed to kill a mob, and these are generally the minimum number of strikes needed. However, you may need fewer strikes if you use the critical hit tactic and more if the opponent wears armor, heals quickly, or if you don't have a fully charged bow.

As with pretty much everything, practice makes perfect. So to become a truly great fighter, get your sword and bow out and start taking out those mobs.

Note: The tips in this book are for the Minecraft PC game 1.8. If you are using a different version of Minecraft, some effects and behaviors may be slightly different. You can research any topic further by visiting the official Minecraft community wiki at Minecraft.gamepedia.com.

CHAPTER : I

SWORDS

Your primary Minecraft combat weapons are, of course, your sword and your bow. Your sword is for close combat, or melee, and your bow is for distance attacks. However, if you are caught unprepared—while harvesting a crop of melons, for example—you can use a tool if you have one; a pickaxe, axe, or shovel will deal more damage than your bare hands. There are other items in Minecraft you can use and build to inflict damage. Flint and steel and a bucket of lava are two popular warfare weapons.

The wooden sword is your first weapon, unless you are lucky and can get to stone quickly with your wooden pickaxe! One of your first goals in Survival mode should be to upgrade to a stone sword. Then continue upgrading until you have a couple of trusty enchanted diamond swords at your side. Left-click with a sword in hand to strike and right-click to block incoming strikes.

Crafting a Sword

You'll need two blocks of a single type of weapons material (wood planks, stone, gold ingot, iron ingot, or diamond ore) and one stick to make a sword. If you are making a wooden sword, you need to use the same kind of wood for both wood planks and the stick.

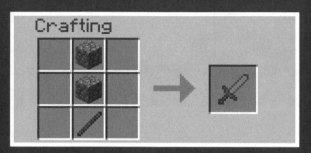

Sword recipe: 2 sword material + 1 stick.

You can also acquire weapons from killed mobs and from trading with villagers. Sometimes a zombie will spawn with a sword in hand or a skeleton may spawn with an enchanted bow. There's a chance they will drop the weapons when they die, and then they're yours.

Sword Damage

The amount of damage a sword can do depends on the material it is made of. Wooden swords deal the least damage, diamond the most. Compare the stats on the next page to using your bare hands, which causes 1 point of damage. Keep in mind that a heart is equal to 2 health points. Also notice that the golden sword gives the same damage as the wooden sword! It often makes sense to go from an iron sword straight to a diamond one, skipping the gold. You can increase the amount of damage you deal by using a critical hit, which you perform by jumping and then striking as you fall. A critical hit increases the damage by up to about 50 percent.

Material	Damage Points/ Hearts
Wooden Sword	5 points ♥♥♥
Stone Sword	6 points ♥♥♥
Iron Sword	7 points or ♥♥♥♥
Golden Sword	5 points ♥♥♥
Diamond Sword	8 points ♥♥♥♥

Sword Durability

Each weapon—and tool—has a limit on its use called its durability. Durability is measured in number of uses. By far the most durable swords are the diamond swords, which can last for more than 1,500 uses. Only your hands can last longer! Meanwhile, gold is not very durable at all and only lasts 33 uses. Once you've used a weapon the maximum number of times, it breaks and disappears. Here are the stats:

Sword Material	Uses
Wooden Sword	60
Stone Sword	132
Iron Sword	251
Golden Sword	33
Diamond Sword	1563

About Durability

Durability is how long a weapon or tool will last—how many chops, stabs, and swings at an item, mob, or player before it breaks. For example, an iron axe has a durability of 251, which means you can use it 251 times. When a weapon or tool breaks, it makes a clanking sound and disappears from your inventory. If you use a tool or weapon on an item it isn't meant for, like using a sword to break a dirt block, it usually counts as two uses rather than one. So it's good to use the right tool for the job, unless you are in a pickle.

You can quickly see how much you've used a weapon by looking at it in your inventory. At the bottom of the weapon's icon is the durability bar. The durability bar only shows up after you've used the weapon or tool for the first time, and it starts as a full green bar. As you use the weapon, the bar shortens and eventually turns red. Finally, the colored bar disappears, leaving an empty gray space when you are at the end of the weapon's lifetime. (However, you still have a couple of uses when the colored bar disappears. The number of uses remaining depends on the material. A gold weapon will have only 2 more uses while a diamond will have 61.

Under the sword, pickaxe, and bow you can see the durability bar.

You can also find out the exact durability remaining on any weapon in your inventory by turning durability tool tips on. To do this, press the F3 and H buttons at the same time. On a Mac, you may need to press the Fn, F3, and H buttons at the same time.

You can see exact durability in item tool tips if you press F3+H to turn this on.

CHAPTER 2

BOW AND ARROW

A bow and arrow is essential for killing mobs from a distance. If you have a chance to kill a mob from a little ways away, take it. This keeps you safe. However, you will still need to get up close to any dropped experience orbs to get the XP points.

Crafting a Bow and an Arrow

The hard part of bows and arrows is getting the resources to make enough of them, especially when you are at the start of your game. You will need three pieces of string, which you get fairly easily from killing spiders with your sword. In the daytime, big spiders are passive, and you can often find a couple spiders in the morning that spawned overnight around your house. They'll turn hostile when you strike your first blow, but at least you start out with the advantage.

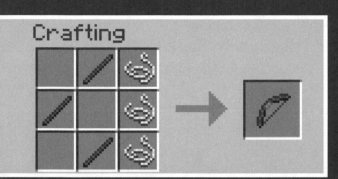

Craft a bow with 3 sticks + 3 string.

For arrows, you *can* gather some already made arrows by killing skeletons. Skeletons will randomly drop 0–2 arrows. However, unless you have a skeleton mob farm, you won't get enough arrows from killing skeletons alone. To make your own arrows, you need sticks, flint, and feathers. A flint, 1 stick, and 1 feather make 4 arrows. Ideally, you'll want to have between a half stack and a stack of arrows (32–64) on you pretty much all the time, depending on how often you use your bow. For 64 arrows, you'll need 16 pieces of flint and 16 feathers. And *that* means you'll need to shovel about 160 blocks of gravel and kill about 16 chickens. (You probably will want the Infinity enchantment for your bow as soon as possible! The Infinity enchantment gives you infinite arrows, as long as you keep one single arrow in your inventory.)

Craft arrows from 1 flint + 1 stick + 1 feather.

You can recover some arrows you have shot that missed their marks and landed in the ground or trees, but these won't be enough to keep you supplied. You can't recover any arrows shot by a skeleton or arrows shot while using the Infinity enchantment.

Bow Durability and Damage

An unenchanted bow will last for 385 uses.

Depending on the strength of your shot (how far you pull the bow back), a bow will cause 1–10 points of damage. You can achieve a critical hit with a bow by pulling it back all the way; this is also called a fully charged bow. The bow will shake a little when fully charged, and the arrow you release will leave a trail of tiny stars. A fully charged arrow can fly as far as 65 blocks. It will give 9 points of damage or, very occasionally, 10.

A fully charged arrow leaves a trail of stars.

Each mob and player in Minecraft has a specified number of health points. Players have 20 health points, and these are represented in your heads-up display (HUD) as hearts. (Your HUD is the set of bars, stats, and inventory hotbar at the bottom of your screen.) A tiny slime block only has 1 point (half a heart) while the Wither boss has 300 points (150 hearts). Once a mob or player has no health points left, they die. When you strike a mob or player, the tool or weapon you use deals a specific amount of damage points. Each damage point takes away 1 health point. In addition to weapons and tools, things that can cause damage to a mob or player include fire, lava, lightning, cactus, TNT explosions, drowning, falling, suffocating, poison, starvation, the Thorns enchantment on another player's armor, the Wither effect, and just being in the Void. The Void is the empty space beyond bedrock. The land of The End is also surrounded by the Void.

Your HUD shows your health status, hunger status, and experience level above your inventory hotbar.

You can repair weapons (or armor) by combining a used item with an identical new or used item on your crafting grid. It doesn't matter in which square of the crafting grid you place the two weapons. However, both weapons must be of the same material. Therefore, you can't combine a stone sword with a diamond one. The resulting weapon has the usage points of both weapons added together. If this totaled durability is less than the maximum durability a new version of the weapon would have, you also get a bonus of up to 5 percent of the total possible durability. To get the most benefit from that 5 percent bonus, repair two worn weapons whose added durability is 95 percent or less than full durability for the weapon. If you don't want to check points and do calculations, all you really have to do is make sure to repair one already worn weapon with another already worn weapon. Both weapons should show some of the green durability bar missing. Be careful not to repair an enchanted weapon on the grid. Doing this will remove the enchantments. To repair an enchanted weapon (or tool), you should use an anvil. See the chapter on enchanted weapons for more information.

Repair two used weapons to get bonus durability.

CHAPTER 3

OTHER WEAPONS

You aren't limited to the standard bow and sword for defeating your foes. You can use an interesting variety of other Minecraft items to damage or kill your enemies. Some are excellent substitutes for your sword or bow.

Tools

Axes, pickaxes, and shovels can deal more damage than your bare fists. Like swords, the weakest and least durable tools are made of wood, and the strongest and most damaging are made of diamond. However, they aren't as durable in combat as they are at their assigned task. If you use a tool rather than a weapon to strike a mob, it will count as two uses in durability, rather than one. Here's a breakdown of what they can do:

	Wood	Stone	Iron	Gold	Diamond
Axe Damage	4.5	5.5	6.5	4.5	7.5
Pickaxe Damage	4	5	6	4	7
Shovel Damage	3.5	4.5	5.5	3.5	6.5
Durability (Pickaxe, Axe, Shovel)	60	132	251	33	1562

Using a hoe is the same as using your hands. It doesn't do any more damage and doesn't register any durability hits if it isn't used to till dirt.

Bucket of Lava

A bucket of lava is essential for your inventory. You do have to be careful about placing the lava, so you aren't damaged as well. It's best to hop up on a quickly placed block of gravel first. Buckets of lava are best poured at the last minute, so that the enemy is close by or doesn't have enough time to react. In the Overworld, lava will flow 3 blocks away from the block you pour it on. It will also burn most items in its path as well as any mob, except in the Nether. Nether mobs are not damaged by either lava or fire. Lava flows faster in the Nether than in the Overworld.

Flint and Steel

Flint and steel is a small tool crafted from an iron ingot and flint (you get flint from shoveling gravel). You place it on a block and right-click it to set it alight. You can use it against mobs by simply clicking the ground under their feet or the blocks in front of them if they are running. You can make a Creeper explode almost immediately by clicking it with flint and steel. Flint and steel has a durability of 65.

Anvil

Anvils are used primarily for repairing and enchanting weapons and armor. However, they have an interesting characteristic that makes them suitable as weapons. They respond to gravity, and if they are dropped from a good height, they will land with a force powerful enough to kill a mob or player. Anvils will cause approximately 2 points of damage per block fallen, up to a maximum of 40 points (20 hearts).

Anvil Traps: For a very simple anvil trap, you can place an anvil on top of a pillar of signs. This will get the anvil up high enough so that it will cause damage when it falls. At the bottom of the pillar, you need to create a way that a mob or player will break the block that the pillar stands on. When they do this, all the signs will drop, and so will the anvil. You must press Shift when you click to place signs (and the anvil) on top of each other like this. You also need to disguise the pillar of signs if you are trying this on other players in a PvP server. For example, the pillar could be just above a block of diamond in a fake mining corridor that you know players will travel down. Any player mining the diamond block from beneath will be hit. As an even simpler alternative, wait on top of a cliff or roof. Place the anvil in the same way you place gravel when you want it to fall—against another block. The anvil will drop heavily to the ground, injuring any player or mob in its way.

Cutaway of a simple anvil trap.

TNT

TNT is an explosive block in Minecraft. It will kill mobs or players close to it. You can find TNT at the bottom of desert temples or craft it from gunpowder (a drop from Creepers) and sand. To set it alight, you use flint and steel. This gives you a few seconds to run before it explodes. TNT can also be ignited with a flaming arrow, lava and fire, traveling over an activator rail in a minecart, a redstone pulse, dispensers, and more. TNT will destroy up to three-quarters of the blocks around it, unless it's in water. In water it won't destroy anything, but it will give an explosive sound. Two popular combat uses for TNT are TNT traps and TNT cannons.

TNT Trap: To make a TNT trap, place the TNT where you want it. Connect TNT to a trigger mechanism, like a pressure plate or a lever. A player or mob stepping on the pressure plate will start the TNT countdown. Or use a lever to ignite the TNT yourself.

Connect a pressure plate to TNT with redstone. You will want to hide the redstone trail, though!

Arrow Dispenser Trap

An automatic arrow dispenser is another common weapon used in a variety of creative ways in Minecraft. For a simple one that dispenses one arrow at a time, use redstone to connect a dispenser to a pressure plate. The pressure plate should be a short distance away from but right in front of the dispenser's mouth. There is an example on the following page. Once you have it working, you can cover up the redstone with other blocks to hide it. This is something you could place in a corridor in your home to deter intruders!

Simple arrow dispenser.

CHAPTER 4

ARMOR

Armor is essential in combat. While you can survive occasional attacks from lesser mobs without it, it is armor that lets you survive big damage attacks and continue fighting. Armor protects you from sword or contact attacks from mobs and other players, as well as from arrows, fire, lava, fishing rods, Ghast or Blaze fire balls, fire charges, cactus damage, and explosions. It doesn't protect you from drowning, suffocating, falling, status effects, extended fire exposure, the Void, or Potions of Harming.

Crafting armor requires 24 pieces of the same material, either leather, gold, iron, or diamond. You can't craft chainmail armor, but you can trade villagers for it. Rarely, a skeleton or zombie wearing chainmail armor will drop it when killed.

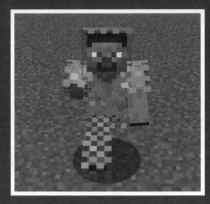

Full suit of chainmail armor.

Each piece of armor provides 1–8 defense points. Each defense point gives a reduction of 4 percent on incoming damage. On your HUD, you can see the total number of defense points your current armor will provide. A chestplate icon is equal to 2 defense points. The separate armor pieces don't protect specific parts of your body, they just add up total defense points. So if you are just starting out and are very poor on materials, you can start with leather boots or a leather helmet. The boots cost 4 leather, whereas it costs 5 leather for the helmet. They both give 1 point of defense, but the boots will last longer. From the charts below, you can work out which pieces of armor you can afford and what will give you the most protection and last the longest.

Protection from Full Sets of Armor

Material	Full Set Protection	Damage Reduction
Leather		28%
Golden		44%
Chain		48%
Iron		60%
Diamond		80%

Individual Armor Defense Points

	Leather	Gold	Chainmail	Iron	Diamond
Helmet	1	2	2	2	3
Chestplate	3	5	5	6	8
Leggings	2	3	4	5	6
Boots	1	1	1	2	3

Durability

Armor durability is lowered by weapon or melee attacks, explosions, lava, and fire. The greatest damage done to your armor is by TNT explosions or Creeper explosions, but you can halve the durability hit by blocking with your sword. Each attack counts as 1 hit, and 1 point will be taken from the durability of each separate piece of armor. Once the durability of armor reaches 0, the bar disappears and you can use it one more time. Also, if you are using armor that reduces damage, the armor will reduce in durability when you take (and it repels) damage.

	Leather	Gold	Chainmail or Iron	Diamond
Helmet	56	78	166	364
Chestplate	81	113	241	529
Leggings	76	106	226	496
Boots	66	92	196	430

With Minecraft 1.8, you can place your armor on armor stands.

Horse Armor

In chests found in dungeons, temples, and mineshafts, as well as village blacksmith shops, you can find horse armor. There are three types of horse armor. Iron armor gives the horse 20 percent protection, gold gives 28 percent, and diamond 44 percent. Although you can't enchant it, horse armor has unlimited durability, so you don't have to repair it.

Horse with diamond armor.

CHAPTER 5

ENCHANTING

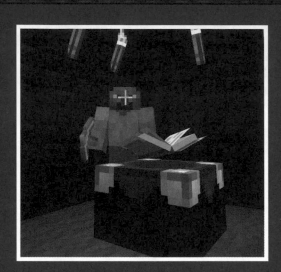

Enchanting and brewing potions aren't easy to do at the beginning of the game. Usually these activities will have to wait until you've gathered the proper resources. However, getting to this level should be a major goal if you want to survive well in Normal or Hard mode. Enchanted weapons and armor make a huge difference in surviving combat, as can potions. They are absolutely necessary for fighting the strongest mobs, like the Ender Dragon and Wither.

Enchanting comes before brewing potions, because you don't have to go to the Nether to start enchanting. To start enchanting, you need an enchantment table, which you craft from obsidian, books, and diamonds, and lapis lazuli to pay for the enchantments. The levels of enchantment you can give to an item are increased by surrounding the table with up to 15 book-shelves. There are different levels for enchantments. For example, a Protection IV enchantment will give more protection than a Protection I enchantment.

Crafting an enchantment table.

To enchant, click on the enchanting table and place the item you want to enchant in the left slot. In the right panel, you'll be given three choices of enchantment. It will tell you how many experience levels you need to perform the enchantment, as well as how much lapis lazuli (and how many experience levels) it will cost. Select the enchantment you want on the right and then remove your enchanted item. Sometimes you will get additional enchantments with the one you picked. Enchanted items have a magical glow.

In the enchanting screen, you can mouse over the three enchanting options for a tooltip that shows what one of the enchantments will be.

The higher your experience level (shown in your green experience bar), the more XP points you need to get to the next level. Because the best enchantments require level 30, you should stop and enchant something whenever you get to level 30. Going from level 27 back to level 30 is faster than going from level 30 to 33.

Armor Enchantments

The **Protection** enchantment reduces any kind of damage. **Fire Protection** reduces damage from fire, and **Blast Protection** reduces damage from explosions. **Projectile Protection** protects you from damage from arrows and Ghast or Blaze fireballs. **Feather Falling** (boots only) reduces damage from falls. **Depth Strider** (boots only) allows you to move more quickly in water. **Respiration** (helmet only) helps you breathe and see under water. **Aqua Affinity** (helmet only) makes it easier to mine underwater. **Thorns** inflicts a small amount of damage on anyone attacking you. Of all these, Protection is often the best, because it gives you general protection from almost everything. However, once you start getting lots of diamonds, you can think about creating different suits for armor for different occasions: visiting the Nether, fighting guardians, or caving.

Enchanted armor can help you move, breathe, and mine underwater.

Sword Enchantments

Sharpness increases damage. **Smite** increases damage more, but only to undead mobs, and **Bane of Arthropods** does the same for spiders, silverfish, and Endermites. **Fire Aspect** will light your target on fire, and **Knockback** will knock him, her, or it back. **Looting** gives a chance of getting better drops from your hostile mobs. Of all these, choose Sharpness over Smite and Bane of Arthropods. Looting is also very helpful for getting those rare drops.

Bow Enchantments

Power increases damage, while **Punch** gives more knockback. **Flame** will send a flaming arrow to deal fire damage. **Infinity** means you need only a single arrow in your inventory to shoot as much as you want. Of all these, choose Infinity if you have any issues with arrow making, and then Power.

Using Gold

It might seem from all the stats that gold is a waste of time as a weapons or tool material. It has terrible durability, and a golden sword doesn't do more damage than the lowly wooden sword. However, gold has a special attribute that you should keep in mind. It is more "enchantable"—you can get better enchantments for the same XP cost as another material. That means you are more likely to get Sharpness IV at your enchanting table with a golden sword than a diamond sword.

Repairing Enchanted Weapons

Anvils allow you to repair an enchanted weapon and keep its enchantments. You do this by placing your worn item on the left and either a new item of the same material on the right or, in some cases, the material the item is made of, like diamond or iron. You can also combine two enchanted weapons of the same material to combine enchantments. An anvil also allows you to combine an unenchanted weapon with an enchanted book to place the book's enchantment on the weapon. If you combine two similar items with the same enchantment level, the resulting item will be given the next level enchantment, if there is a next level. For example, you can combine two Sharpness IV swords to make a Sharpness V sword.

Repairing with the anvil will also cost experience levels; here it is just one level.

Potions will help you in battle tremendously. They can restore your health, make you invisible, or make you faster and stronger. They are a must when you are fighting boss mobs like the Wither. You will be ready to start making potions when you start visiting the Nether and killing the mobs there, as they supply much of what you need. For example, to make a brewing stand, you'll need a Blaze rod dropped by a Blaze. When you have drunk a potion, a notice shows up on your inventory screen along with how long the potion will last, if it isn't an instant potion.

Brewing

First you brew bottles of water and another ingredient to create a "base" potion. This ingredient is almost always Nether wart, and this brew is called the Awkward Potion. Then you brew your base potion with a new ingredient to make a primary potion, which will give the drinker a special status effect, like Speed, for a certain amount of time.

Brewing the Awkward Potion with Nether wart and water.

Then, if you want, you can brew your primary potion again with a modifying ingredient to create a secondary potion. Use glowstone to make the effect stronger, gunpowder to make it into a splash potion, or redstone to make the potion's effect last longer. Glowstone and redstone cancel each other's effect. In many cases, you can add fermented spider eye to a potion to reverse its effects and make it into a harming potion.

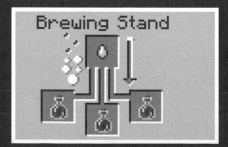

Brewing the Potion of Regeneration with a Ghast tear and the Awkward Potion base.

Modifying the Potion of Regeneration by brewing it with gunpowder to make a splash potion.

With a splash potion, you can use the potion as a weapon. The splash potion looks a little like a grenade, with a pin at the top. Splash potions are much more effective when they are thrown at the hitbox of the mob or player, rather than an adjacent block, like the block the mob is standing on. Think of the hitbox as an invisible box around an entity or item that defines where it can be struck or clicked on. Be careful of using potions on the undead, though. On skeletons, zombies, and the like, splash potions can work in reverse. A Potion of Harming will heal a skeleton, a Potion of Healing will harm it, and a Potion of Regeneration won't have any effect. The undead, spiders, and the Ender Dragon also won't be affected by poisonous potions.

Basic Potions and Ingredients

Awkward (Base Potion)	Water and Nether Wart
Fire Resistance	Magma Cream
Healing	Glistering Melon

Leaping	Rabbit's Foot
Night Vision	Golden Carrot
Poison	Spider Eye
Regeneration	Ghast Tear
Strength	Blaze Powder
Swiftness	Sugar
Water Breathing	Pufferfish
Harming	Potion of Water Breathing or Poison + Fermented Spider Eye
Slowness	Potion of Swiftness or Fire Resistance + Fermented Spider Eye
Weakness	Doesn't Use Awkward Potion as a Base, Just Water with Fermented Spider Eye

CHAPTER 7

FIGHTING TECHNIQUES

You can improve your combat skills by practicing some basic techniques. Certain techniques work better for specific situations than others.

Blocking: You can prevent up to 50 percent of damage from an incoming strike by right-clicking to block the attack.

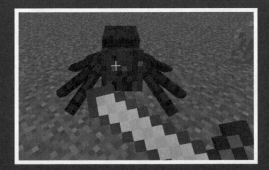

Right-click with your sword to block damage from incoming attacks.

Block-Hitting: To block-hit with your sword, click right and left at same time, or alternate between these two. This can help you keep striking quickly while still protecting against your opponent's strikes. However, when you block you are moving slower, so this tactic is best used when you don't anticipate having to run around. Also, if your opponent can't see you, they can't hit you, so there's no need to block-hit when you are behind someone, for example.

Knockback: To knock-back an opponent, sprint to them and hit them while sprinting. This can knock a player back almost twice as far as regular hit. The only mobs you don't want to use this against are skeletons (this can give them time to recharge their bows) and any mob that you have difficulty catching.

Encircling: Circle around your enemy. This makes it harder for them to hit you. If you can keep behind the other player or mob, you can deliver damage while they can't.

Critical Hits: When you are falling through the air, you deliver up to 50 percent more damage to foes. Jump, and as you fall, strike. You can practice these as you slaughter your herd of cows or pigs.

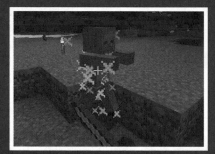

Jump, then strike as you fall for a critical hit, which will show stars around your foe.

Strafing: If your enemy is using a bow or other projectiles, use your A and D keys to move left and right as you approach your enemy to make it harder for them to hit you.

Sword Timing: Check your sword timing. If you click very fast, Minecraft's sword animation can't keep up with your speed. When you see this happening, the game is dropping some of your sword hit clicks to keep up. If it's not animating a click, your sword isn't damaging your opponent. If you click a little slower, you can see that for each click, an animation occurs, and each click will count. This can actually improve your clicking/hitting rate.

Aiming: When you aim with your bow (or with any projectile), take into account the direction your opponent is moving. If they are moving to your right, aim a little right, so they walk into your arrow. If you are waiting for an opponent to come into view, prepare by charging your bow, and keeping it extended, until they appear and you can shoot a critical arrow hit, practically before they even notice you. If you are fighting up close and using your arrow, you may not have time to fully charge your bow. Charge it halfway by pulling for a couple counts and then shooting and recharging.

Arrows fall as they fly, so aim above your target. Practice will help make you perfect.

Stunning with Fishing Rods: Many Minecraft PvP warriors like to use fishing rods in combat. Right-clicking your opponent as you run toward or away from them stuns them for a moment, allowing you more time to attack them or to escape.

Hide Surprise Weapons: If you are about to use flint and steel, or a bucket of lava, don't hold it until the last minute. When you hold it, your opponent will see it in your hands and know what you are about to do. This can give them a chance to escape. Use the number keys on top of your keyboard, 1–9, to switch quickly between weapons.

Ender Pearl Escape: You can use Ender Pearls to teleport anywhere you can aim the Pearl. It will damage you slightly, but much less than a fall from a height, a fall into lava, or a melee in which you are outgunned or outnumbered.

Water Fighting: If you can get your opponent into water, that will slow them down. If you are both in water, get below them. Your reach is longer from this angle than from the position above, so you can avoid their swings while still hitting them.

Keep Eating: Your hunger level is the most important thing in making sure you heal quickly. Make sure you have plenty of good food, like steaks or baked potatoes, to eat when your hunger drops.

Practice: Set up a world where your only goal is to fight, die, and fight again. If you turn cheats on, you can use Creative mode to gather armor, food, weapons, and more into chests. That way, when you switch to Hard mode, you won't have to spend time roasting that cow and can concentrate on fighting.

CHAPTER 8
THE MOBS YOU FIGHT

T he word *mob* is short for mobile. Mobile was used in early multiple-player gaming to describe any entity that could move.

Mob Types

In Minecraft, mobs can be classed in several ways, like how aggressive they are or where they spawn.

Passive mobs, like chickens, will never attack you; other passive mobs include bat, chicken, cow, horse, mooshroom, ocelot, pig, rabbit, sheet, squid, and villager.

Neutral mobs are passive except in certain circumstances, when they become hostile. Neutral mobs are the cave spider (at high light levels), Enderman, spider (at high light levels), wolf, and zombie pigman.

Hostile mobs, like Creepers, attack you without being provoked. They include the Blaze, baby zombie, chicken jockey, Creeper, Elder Guardian, Endermite, Ghast, Guardian, Killer Bunny, magma cube, silverfish, skeleton, slime, spider jockey, witch, Wither, Wither skeleton, zombie, and zombie villager.

Darkness mobs spawn in low light levels in the Overworld. Darkness mobs include the Enderman, skeleton, Creeper, spider, and zombie.

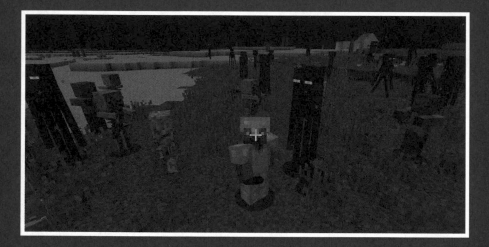

The Darkness mobs come out at night.

Nether mobs spawn only in the Nether. Nether mobs include the Ghast, magma cube, and zombie pigman.

Local mobs spawn in specific areas in the Overworld or Nether. Overworld local mobs are cave spiders, slimes, silverfish, and witches. Nether local mobs are Wither skeletons and Blazes.

Utility mobs are mobs that were created to serve. Iron and snow golems are utility mobs. Iron golems can spawn naturally in large villages, and protect villagers by attacking hostile mobs. Snow golems can only be created by the player, and they also attack most mobs.

Iron and snow golems can help you out in a pinch.

Boss mobs have a more complicated programming than other types of mobs and are able to heal themselves. They have very high levels of health and attack strengths, so they are difficult to kill. Boss mobs include the Ender Dragon and the Wither.

Hostile Mob Behavior

Hostile mobs spawn within 24–128 blocks of a player. Most can see any player that is within 16 blocks of them; some can see further. When a mob sees the player in its line of sight (there are no opaque blocks in the way), it begins to pursue the player. If a hostile mob is 128 blocks away from a player, it will despawn or disappear. However, if you put a nametag on a mob, it won't despawn. Some hostile mobs can spawn with or pick up weapons and armor, and if they have these, they also won't despawn.

Once they spawn, they walk around randomly. However, if there is no player nearby (within 32 blocks), they'll stop walking after about 5 seconds and just stand still.

Almost all mobs are vulnerable to the same things players are: drowning, lava, suffocation, cactus, TNT explosions, and fall damage. Mobs are also damaged by fire, except for Nether mobs, who live in the fiery biome of Hell and are used to such things.

Almost all mobs are vulnerable to the same kinds of damage players are. These Creepers have been caught in lava.

CHAPTER 9
BABY ZOMBIES AND CHICKEN JOCKEYS

Baby Zombies

aby zombies are miniature zombies. There are baby versions of zombies, zombie villagers, and zombie pigmen, and they all behave pretty much exactly the same way. About 5 percent of zombies spawn as baby zombies. The drops the babies give are the same as for their adult version. They can be equipped and pick up armor or weapons like the adults.

A baby zombie villager and a baby zombie pigman.

Chicken Jockeys

A chicken jockey is a baby zombie, baby zombie villager, or baby zombie pigman riding a chicken. They are very rare. There is a 5 percent chance that a baby zombie will spawn as a chicken jockey. This works out to a 0.25 percent chance for a chicken jockey to spawn. That's means about 1 in every 400 zombies will be a chicken jockey. However, if there are chickens nearby when the baby zombie spawns, its chance of becoming a chicken jockey are almost doubled.

A chicken jockey.

Baby zombies and chicken jockeys may be cute, but they're harder to fight than the slow adults. They are very fast!

If the baby's riding a chicken, you can't kill it by pushing it over a cliff. The chicken can just flutter slowly down to the ground without it or its rider being harmed. If a chicken jockey comes into contact with flowing water, it separates into the baby zombie and the chicken.

BABY ZOMBIE STATS

Mob Type: Hostile, Darkness

Health: Chicken – 4

Baby Zombie – 20

Attack Strength:

Easy – 2

Normal – 9

Hard – 13

Experience: Up to 22 (12 for baby zombie; 10 for a chicken)

Drops: Rotten flesh, 1 raw chicken, 0–2 feathers, more rarely 1 carrot, 1 potato, any armor or weapons it holds, 1 iron ingot, or 1 gold ingot (for a baby zombie pigman)

Spawn: Baby zombies and chicken jockeys spawn in the Overworld at light level 7 or below. Baby zombie pigmen spawn in the Nether.

Sword Strikes to Kill (Baby Zombie):

Wood: 4

Stone: 4

Iron: 3

Gold: 4

Diamond: 3

Bow Strikes to Kill: 3

Fighting a Baby Zombie or Chicken Jockey

To fight these kids, you will need to use your sword, because they run so fast. They are pretty hilarious, but if you don't pay attention they can still kill you. Although they spawn at low light levels, they don't burn in daylight, and they can also run through 1x1-block gaps. The best way to defeat a chicken jockey or baby zombie, once it has set its mark on you, is to attack as fast as you can. If you can, get two straight blocks above the baby zombie (by pillaring with two blocks of gravel, for example) and strike it from there.

CHAPTER 10

BLAZE

Blazes are hostile mobs found in Nether fortresses. They have a body made of dark gray smoke surrounded by three sections of four whirling golden rods. They are fierce opponents. Once they see you, they fly up in the air, catch on fire for a moment, and then rapidly hurl three fire charges at you. They'll repeat these actions over and over again. While it might seem best to avoid blazes entirely, they drop blaze rods, which are essential for several Minecraft activities. You need one blaze rod to make a brewing station for potion, and blaze powder makes the Potion of Fire Resistance. You also need blaze powder to make Eyes of Ender, which you are required to find and repair the End portal.

Blazes can spawn randomly in Nether fortresses, but you will also find special rooms in a fortress that house Blaze spawners. These rooms are up a short flight of stairs and have short walls topped by Nether fence.

A Blaze spawner in a Nether fortress.

BLAZE STATS

Mob type: Hostile, Nether, Local

Health: 20

Attack Strength (Fire Charges):

Easy – 3

Normal – 5

Hard – 7

Attack Strength (From Contact):

> Easy – 4 🖤🖤
>
> Normal – 6 🖤🖤🖤
>
> Hard – 9 🖤🖤🖤🖤🖤

Experience: 10

Drops: 0–1 Blaze rods (in console edition may drop 0–2 glowstone dust)

Spawn: In Nether fortresses randomly or through a Blaze spawner, at low light levels (11 or less)

Sword Strikes to Kill:

🗡 Wood: 4, but don't bother if you don't have armor and strong swords. Unless you're on Easy, you'll be quickly overpowered and killed by fire damage, both from the fire charges and from contact by the Blazes.

🗡 Stone: 4

🗡 Iron: 4

🗡 Gold: 4

🗡 Diamond: 3

Fighting the Blaze

The Blaze is one of the more difficult mobs to fight. It flies up and down and back and forth, often out of reach. It fires its charges at you very quickly, and when it is on fire itself, it will give you significant fire damage when it touches you. A fire resistance potion will protect you greatly from the Blaze. However, to make potions, you first need a Blaze rod to create a brewing station. So if you have not killed any Blazes yet, you will not be able to make potions. In this case, you can use an enchanted golden apple, which gives you several status effects for a short time, including Absorption, Regeneration, Resistance, and five minutes of Fire Resistance.

After hurling its charges, the Blaze needs a few seconds to recharge.

Surprisingly, snowballs are a pretty good tactic to use against Blazes. Snowballs only do damage to two mobs, the Blaze and the Ender Dragon. They deliver 3 points of damage to the Blaze and 1 to the Dragon. A common tactic is to throw snowballs at the Blaze initially, and then run in with your sword to kill it. If you have Fire Resistance from a potion, you can also try hooking it with a fishing rod to bring it close and then attack with your sword. Blazes are also damaged by water, but water sizzles and disappears in the Nether.

Once a Blaze spawns, you have a few seconds while it gets ready to deliver the fire charges. After it hurls the charges (which it will only do if you are in its line of sight and within 16 blocks), it will take another few seconds to recharge. Use these moments to deliver as much damage as you can. If you can hide behind a block, you can pop out to draw the blaze's fire, hide again to dodge the charges, then come back out to attack during the short lull. However, this is much harder to do when you have multiple Blazes bearing down on you!

You can also create a space whereby you are below the Blaze, protected by blocks such as Nether brick, with just a one block gap that allows you to strike the Blaze with your sword. If another mob, like a Wither skeleton, is nearby, hide behind it. If you are lucky, the Blaze will hit the skeleton, which will then attack the Blaze. Once they are engaged, you can attack the Blaze yourself.

CHAPTER II
CAVE SPIDER

Like their larger cousin, the spider, the cave spider is a neutral mob in light levels of 12 and above, and hostile at lower levels. It looks just like a regular spider, but it has a bluish fur and is smaller and faster. It is also poisonous on Normal and Hard difficulty levels. However, they don't spawn naturally like other mobs, they only spawn from spawners found in abandoned mineshafts. You can identify a cave spider spawner by the masses of cobwebs surrounding it. These mob spawners themselves look like a cage the size of a block with a miniature mob spinning around inside. Cave spiders, like spiders, can climb blocks vertically, like climbing a ladder.

Cave spiders are smaller than the regular spider, taking up less than a full 1x1 block of space. This means they can fit through a space as small as a block wide and a half block tall. Because of their small size and speed, they can be difficult to defeat.

CAVE SPIDER STATS

Mob Type: Neutral, Local

Health: 12 pts ❤❤❤❤❤❤

Attack strength:

      Easy – 2 ❤

      Normal – 2 (with venom) ❤

      Hard – 3 (with venom) ❤❤

Experience: 5 pts

Drops: 0–2 string, 0–1 spider eye

Spawn: Spawn in abandoned mineshafts only, at low light levels

Sword Strikes to Kill:

    Wood: 3

    Stone: 2

    Iron: 2

    Gold: 3

    Diamond: 2

    Bow Strikes to Kill: 2

Fighting the Cave Spider

To defeat the cave spider, you need to kill existing and spawning spiders and disable or destroy the spawner itself. Because they are so fast, you will be using a sword against them instead of the bow, which takes several moments to pull and charge before you can fire an arrow.

You will find yourself trying to battle these spiders at the same time as trying to destroy enough cobwebs around the spawner so that you can disable it. You can use a bucket of water to remove cobwebs, and shears are the fastest tool to cut them. Water will also uproot any torches placed on the ground, so be aware of where your torches are. One tactic is to close off the ends of the corridor they are in, and then tunnel in just above or below the spawner, so you can quickly destroy it with your pickaxe or place torches on each side. Placing torches will create enough light that it prevents spiders from spawning, disabling it.

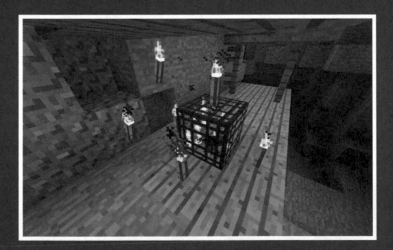

Disarming a cave spider spawner.

Try to avoid letting these spiders get above you, where they can jump on you and damage you. The venom from their bite will cause you enough damage to bring you down to a half-heart of health. It won't kill you, but it will leave you very vulnerable to dying from anything else. Once you are bitten, retreat and use potions or milk to heal before you strike again. If you don't care about losing the spawner or any drops and experience points, you can pour a bucket of lava on it.

CHAPTER 12

CREEPER

Creepers are one of the four main hostile mobs you encounter in the Overworld. The other three are skeletons, spiders, and zombies. Creepers are mottled green, have four tiny rectangular legs, and spawn in low light levels. Unlike zombies and skeletons, they don't die in the sunlight—although we all wish they would.

The biggest problem with Creepers is their silence. You can hear a zombie's groans and the scritching sound of a spider, but Creepers are very nearly silent. If you are lucky, you may hear a little rustle. But unless you are facing toward them as they approach, the last thing you will hear is the sizzle of a fuse burning before the Creeper explodes a block away from you, taking you down with it.

If the Creeper has been hit by lightning, it becomes the even deadlier charged Creeper. A charged Creeper has a bluish tinge flowing around it to signify the electric charge. Its explosion causes more damage than a TNT explosion.

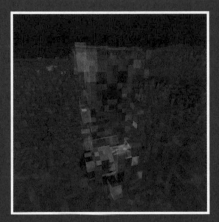

A charged Creeper.

Once either type of Creeper spots you (you have to be within 16 blocks), it will chase you. When it is within a block of you, it will start to sizzle and swell. And once it starts to sizzle, it will explode in 1.5 seconds. If you get away from it (about 3–5 blocks, depending on your difficulty level) within 1 second, the Creeper will not explode.

A swelling Creeper on the left and an exploding Creeper on the right.

CREEPER STATS

Mob Type: Hostile, Darkness

Health: 20 ♥♥♥♥♥♥♥♥♥♥

Attack Strength (Maximum):

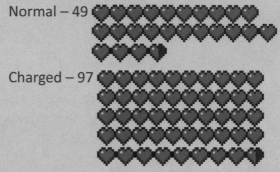

Normal – 49

Charged – 97

Drops: 0–2 gunpowder, a music disc (if killed by a skeleton), and a Creeper head (if killed by a charged Creeper).

Spawn: In the Overworld at light levels of 7 and below.

Sword Strikes to Kill:

Wood: 4

Stone: 4

Iron: 4

Gold: 4

Diamond: 3

Bow Strikes to Kill: 3

Fighting the Creeper

The best way to kill a Creeper is with your bow and arrow, keeping well away from it. If you can't do this, sprint straight to the Creeper and strike it with your sword. Striking it while you sprint will knock it back more than if you don't sprint. The moment you hit the Creeper, press S to move backward immediately. It is better to move backward after you've knocked the Creeper back, rather than try to angle left or right. If you move forward, you will still be too close to it. You can also do this maneuver without sprinting, but the timing is more critical. In either case, repeat the swoop in, smack back, and swoop out procedure until the Creeper dies. You may want to practice ahead of time switching quickly from the W key to move forward and the S key to move back.

As with most mob killing, the best sword enchantment for Creeper killing is Sharpness and the best bow enchantment is Power. If you can add knock back via the Knockback (sword) or Punch (bow) enchantment, that is also a big help, especially for the swoop in and out tactic.

CHAPTER 13

ELDER GUARDIAN

The Elder Guardian (a larger, more powerful version of the Guardian) is an ocean-dwelling hostile mob that appears with a new ocean monument structure. There are three Elder Guardians spawned with each ocean monument, and they will not respawn if you kill them. They live inside the monument. One is in a top room near the monument's treasure (8 gold blocks, hidden by prismarine blocks); the other two live in rooms on opposite wings of the monument.

You can find the rare ocean monument in deep ocean.

The Elder Guardian is very similar to the Guardian; it attacks in the same way, by laser and its defensive spines, but it deals more damage. It gives the same drops with one additional possibility, the wet sponge. Also like the Guardian, it swims suddenly and quickly and attacks both players and squid. Guardians will swim away from an approaching player to gain some range for its laser beam. However, the Elder Guardian has the unique ability to inflict players within a 50-block radius with Mining Fatigue III for five minutes. This is a status effect that will really slow down your mining, making it very difficult to break blocks. When the mob inflicts you with this, you'll see a shadowy image of the Elder Guardian on your screen for a moment.

ELDER GUARDIAN STATS

Mob Type: Hostile, Local

Health: 80

Attack Strength:

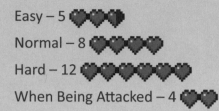

Easy – 5

Normal – 8

Hard – 12

When Being Attacked – 4

Experience: 10

Drops: 0–1 raw fish, 0–2 prismarine shards, 0–1 prismarine crystals, 0–1 wet sponges; more rarely, it will drop raw salmon, clownfish, or pufferfish.

Spawn: Spawns only at an ocean monument, and only once with each ocean monument. Unlike other hostile mobs, they don't despawn, except in Peaceful level.

Sword Strikes to Kill:

Wood: 16

Stone: 14

Iron: 12

Gold: 16

Diamond: 10

Bow Strikes to Kill: 9

Fighting the Elder Guardian

As with fighting the Guardian, you will need to prepare your armor and potions for fighting and moving underwater: Aqua Affinity, Respiration, and Depth Strider enchantments, and Potions of Swiftness, Night Vision, and Water Breathing. You can also use Potion of Invisibility to prevent the Guardians from seeing and attacking you; this is a good tactic.

The Elder Guardian will inflict you with mining fatigue to prevent you from mining to find the hidden blocks of gold.

Like fighting the Guardian, your best move is to attack quickly and attack hard with your sharpest enchanted sword. Because of the Mining Fatigue, you likely won't be able to mine to find the gold blocks hidden in the middle of the monument, so your first goal is to take out the three Elder Guardians.

CHAPTER 14

ENDER DRAGON

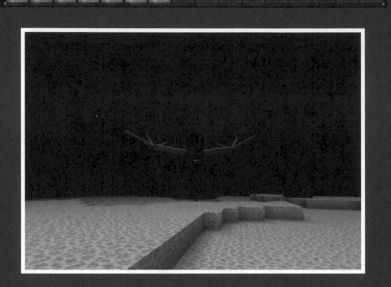

The Ender Dragon is a large black dragon with reddish purple eyes. It is the largest mob in the game, over 20 blocks long. There is only one Ender Dragon, and it is found in the End, a world you travel to through the End portal.

The End is an island made of a special block called End stone, and tall columns of obsidian rise from the ground. The island floats in an endless dark space called the Void. If you fall off the edges of the island and into the Void, you will die. The Ender Dragon flies among the tops of several obsidian columns that have special blocks of crystals on top of them. These crystals regenerate the Dragon's health when it is injured, making it very difficult to slay the Dragon.

When the Ender Dragon is close to you, its purple health bar appears at the top of your screen. When it attacks you, the Ender Dragon flies right at you. It destroys all blocks besides obsidian and End stone in its path and causes damage to you when it hits you, as well as knocks you back. It may fly off for a little while, but will return to attack you again.

ENDER DRAGON STATS

Mob Type: Boss

Health: 200 ♥♥♥♥♥♥♥♥♥♥

Attack Strength:

Easy – 6 ♥♥♥

Normal – 10 ♥♥♥♥♥

Hard – 15 ♥♥♥♥♥♥♥♥

Experience: 12,000

Drops: Dragon egg

Spawn: Only once, in the End

Sword Strikes to Kill:

Wood: 40 (These Strikes to Kill stats are purely theoretical. Because of the way the Ender Dragon heals itself and flies quickly, you will need an enchanted diamond sword and enchanted bow to kill the Dragon, and you may strike many more times than this in the game, because you will miss often.)

Stone: 34

Iron: 29 •

Gold: 40

Diamond: 25

Bow Strikes to Kill: 23

Fighting the Ender Dragon

Before you go to the End, you must be prepared. First, you want to make the portal room safe and place chests to hold extra supplies. Then place a bed and sleep there to reset your spawn point. That way, if you die without killing the Dragon, you can enter the End again quickly with new supplies.

For supplies, you will need enchanted diamond armor, diamond swords, and enchanted bows. Plan on bringing an extra set of armor, three swords, and three bows. Because you will be fighting for a long time, you need several stacks of arrows or the Infinity enchantment on the bow. You will also want to bring at least a stack of obsidian to create a bridge from your spawn point to the main island and safe platforms. In addition to plenty of food, other supplies to consider are several stacks of snowballs, the makings for an army of iron and snow golems, and Potions of Healing and Regeneration.

To fight the Ender Dragon you must first destroy its healing crystals, which are on top of obsidian pillars. They look like cubes rotating in fire. You can also tell a crystal is present when a damaged Dragon flies by one and the crystal emits a ray to heal it. To destroy the crystal, you can throw any projectile at it, even projectiles that don't do damage. You can use your bow and arrow or throw snowballs or eggs. If you hit the crystal, it explodes with more force than TNT, so you don't want to be close! You may want to climb other obsidian pillars and make a safe ledge area using obsidian to fire on other crystals.

These crystals heal the Dragon, making it very difficult to kill. You'll have to destroy these first.

You will also have to deal with hordes of Endermen wandering around. You don't want to provoke them by looking at them, but it's easy to make a mistake. To prevent them from seeing you look at them, you can wear a pumpkin as a helmet. However, this also limits your ability to see well. To keep them occupied, you can unleash armies of iron and snow golems who will attack Endermen automatically and distract them. You could use a Potion of Invisibility, but this doesn't work on the Ender Dragon and you also need to remove your armor for it to work.

Once you've destroyed the crystal, it is time to take on the Ender Dragon. The best weapon to use is the bow. Wait until the Dragon is heading for you, and shoot for its head. Shooting the Dragon's head causes full damage. If you shoot it anywhere else, you will only give the Dragon about a quarter of the damage from your bow. You will need to do this over and over again, healing yourself as you get damaged. The Ender Dragon is immune to lava, potions, and fire. You can only damage the Ender Dragon with explosions or your sword or bow.

When you damage the Dragon, it flies off for a short while, and you can use this time to regroup and heal.

When you finally kill the Dragon, it explodes with impressive flashing rays. Its death creates an End exit portal for you to travel back to the Overworld, as well as a Dragon egg. The Dragon egg doesn't do anything itself. If you click it, it will teleport several blocks away, so it is very difficult to gather. (Hint: If you can get it to drop on a torch, it will turn into a collectible item.)

A dying Ender Dragon.

The End is a dark land, like the Nether, populated only by Endermen and the Ender Dragon. To get there, you must first find a portal, which is in a stronghold. Strongholds are complex mazes of dungeon-like rooms, corridors, and stairways, and there are only three in the Overworld. You'll find prison cells, libraries, and fountain rooms in a stronghold. To find a stronghold, you first gather fifteen or so Ender Pearls by killing Endermen. You craft these into Eyes of Ender using Blaze powder. (You can also trade with villagers for Eyes of Ender.) When you throw an Eye of Ender into the air, it will move in the direction of the nearest stronghold and then drop back to the ground. Pick up the Eye and travel in the direction it pointed. Every so often, throw another Eye into the sky to check your direction. When you are directly over the stronghold, the Eye you throw will fall and sink down into the ground. Now you dig! Once you reach the brick walls of the stronghold, you must break through and find the portal room, which has a silverfish spawner and a broken portal in it. The portal has places for Eyes of Ender to go in 12 frames along its border, but many are missing. You place your Eyes of Ender in the frames to fix the portal. Then you can jump in to travel to the End. Be prepared—the first time you visit the End you can return to the Overworld only by dying or killing the Dragon.

CHAPTER 15

ENDERMAN

ndermen are 3-block-tall black mobs with very long arms and legs. They wander about the Overworld and the End in their own little clouds of purple stars and occasionally pick up a block and hold it. (They're the reason your Minecraft neighborhood has all those little one-block holes in the ground!) They are neutral unless you provoke them, which happens by merely looking at them anywhere from their upper legs to their head. Moving the crosshair over these parts is considered looking, so it's not terribly difficult to avoid them, at least in the Overworld. You can look at their legs without a problem. There are so many Endermen in the End that avoiding looking at them is much more difficult.

ENDERMAN STATS

Mob Type: Neutral, Darkness

Health: 40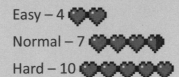

Attack Strength:

Easy – 4

Normal – 7

Hard – 10

Experience: 5

Drops: 0–1 Ender Pearls, used to make Eyes of Ender

Spawn: In light levels of 7 and less in the Overworld and in the End world

Sword Strikes to Kill:

Wood: 8

Stone: 7

Iron: 6

Gold: 8

Diamond: 5

Bow Strikes to Kill: 5

Fighting the Enderman

When you provoke an Enderman by looking at it or by attacking it, it will shudder and shake and make a very unsettling and long groan, like a disturbed airplane. It will teleport toward you suddenly and damage you by contact. When you attack it and it receives damage, it will teleport away and then back to you again, often behind you.

You can't use a bow, other projectiles, or a splash Potion of Harming on an Enderman, as it will teleport away before contact is made.

However, the Enderman has several weaknesses that you can use to your advantage.

- It can't pass under gaps less than three blocks high.

- Usually it doesn't teleport if you attack its lower legs.

- Contact with water causes damage.

- It becomes neutralized by damage from rain, lava, or sunlight.

If you are on the hunt for Ender Pearls and need to kill Endermen, make a little outpost with a 2-block high, 2-block deep gap you can fit into. Stare at an Enderman and nip into your outpost, keeping your back at the wall. When it teleports to you, attack only its legs with your sword. You'll get very little damage, if any, and quite possibly an Ender Pearl out of the deal.

You can defeat Endermen pretty easily by staying in a 2-block high gap and striking their feet.

You can also pillar 3 blocks up, stare at an Enderman, and strike it with your sword when it teleports close by. It can't teleport to your block or fly, so you can swing at it at your leisure. However, it's harder to swing just at its legs, so it may teleport away, leaving you Ender Pearl free.

CHAPTER 16

ENDERMITE

The Endermite is a new mob that came in the Minecraft 1.8 Bountiful Update. Its body is based a little on the silverfish. They look like tail-less, chubby, purple silverfish and, like the silverfish, they are low in health and attack damage. They can also jump up a block like silverfish, suffocate on soul sand, and make similar death squeals. As of 1.8, they only spawn rarely, when you use an Ender Pearl or when an Enderman teleports away. There may be changes to the Endermite in future updates, so keep an eye out!

ENDERMITE STATS

Mob Type: Hostile

Health: 8 ♥♥♥♥

Attack Strength: 2 ♥

Experience: 3

Drops: None

Spawn: There is a 5 percent chance that an Endermite will spawn when you throw an Ender Pearl. They can also spawn when an Enderman teleports away.

Sword Strikes to Kill:

Wood: 2

Stone: 2

Iron: 2

Gold: 2

Diamond: 1

Bow Strikes to Kill: 1

Fighting the Endermite

You can fight the Endermite with your sword at close quarters without having too much harm done to you. A few sword strikes will do it in, and it won't call any pals to help it out. However, they despawn after only a few minutes.

CHAPTER 17

GHAST

The Ghast is one of the largest mobs in Minecraft, with a body that is 4x4 blocks tall and 9 long, hanging tentacles. They float in the sky of the Nether, and if they see you and you are close enough, they will open their mouths to emit a fireball aimed right at you. You can tell if a Ghast is around by the mewling, catlike cry it makes. Like other Nether creatures, they are not damaged by fire or lava.

GHAST STATS

Mob Type:	Hostile, Nether
Health:	10 ❤❤❤❤❤
Attack Strength:	Max 17 ❤❤❤❤❤❤❤❤❤❤
	Damage depends on how far away

the Ghast is and where the player
is in the explosion radius.

Experience: 5

Drops: 0–2 gunpowder, 0–1 Ghast tears

Spawn: In the Nether.

Sword Strikes to Kill:

Wood: 2

Stone: 2

Iron: 2

Gold: 2

Diamond: 2

Bow Strikes to Kill: 1–2

Fighting the Ghast

The Ghast can shoot from a very long range—up to 100 blocks—
but it won't shoot its fireballs at you unless it has line of sight
to you. The fireballs aren't very fast, so you have some time to
hide, if that's what you want to do.

Otherwise, fire up your bow, as that is the easiest way to kill a
Ghast. They don't usually come too close. To protect yourself,
you can build a cobblestone or obsidian wall to nip behind. As
the Ghast fires at you, the fireballs will catch Netherrack near
you on fire, and this is almost as dangerous. If you can create a

cobblestone area to fight from, this can help. If the Ghast is far away, make sure to aim high.

You can also bounce its fireball right back at the Ghast. The fireball travels slowly, so you have enough time to punch it back with your bow or your sword. You can even use your fist and not be damaged or shoot an arrow at the fireball. If you aim the punch just right, you can send the fireball right back to the Ghast, killing it *and* getting the achievement Return to Sender.

A Ghast opens its eyes and mouth right before firing.

It is difficult to get the Ghast drop, a Ghast tear. This is used to make the very handy Potion of Regeneration. Typically, the Ghast will be flying over lava when your arrow hits it, and its drops will land in the lava and burn up. One solution is to hook the Ghast with your fishing rod, draw it toward you, and then attack it with your sword once it is over land. Use a sword enchanted with Looting to maximize your plunder.

CHAPTER 18

GUARDIAN

The Guardian is a brand new mob introduced with the Minecraft 1.8 Bountiful Update. It and the Elder Guardian are the only two hostile mobs of the sea. Guardians spawn nearby a new structure called the ocean monument. An ocean monument is similar to the desert temple and jungle temple, although there are no chests inside. There is a central treasure room in the ocean monument, where 8 gold blocks are hidden behind dark prismarine blocks.

GUARDIAN STATS

Mob Type: Hostile, Local

Health: 30 ♥♥♥♥♥♥♥♥♥♥♥♥♥♥♥

Attack Strength:

Easy – 4

Normal – 6

Hard – 9

Experience: 10

Drops: 1–2 raw fish, 0–2 prismarine shards, 0–1 prismarine crystals.

Spawn: In the ocean by ocean monuments.

Sword Strikes to Kill:

Wood: 6

Stone: 5

Iron: 5

Gold: 6

Diamond: 4

Bow Strikes to Kill: 4

Fighting the Guardian

Because you'll be fighting underwater, you will need to prepare armor and potions that will help you breathe, see, and move quickly beneath the ocean surface.

The Guardian swims suddenly and quickly in and around its ocean monument, attacking players and squid. It attacks by firing its laser at you. However, first it must charge its laser; while this is happening, the laser is purple and does no damage. Then, when it is fully charged, the beam turns yellow, delivers its blow, and stops. A few seconds pass before the Guardian can recharge. The laser can reach about 15 blocks to hit you, as long as there are no solid blocks between the Guardian and you. In addition, if you attack the Guardian while its spikes are out, it will deal you 2 points of damage.

Guardians zap you with rays to damage you.

Wearing armor and enchanted armor can help protect you from the Guardian's laser. It might seem best to stay at a distance and use your bow and arrow. However, arrows don't travel well underwater, and the Guardian moves quickly. It can easily dart out of the way and zap you. Your best tactic is to be aggressive and fast. Corner the Guardian so that it can't escape you, and attack it quickly with the sharpest sword you have.

CHAPTER 19

KILLER BUNNY

The Killer Bunny is a type of rabbit, a new mob introduced with the Minecraft 1.8 Bountiful Update. Rabbits themselves are passive mobs, of course. As you might expect, they are skilled at hopping and eating carrots. The Killer Bunny is spawned very rarely and randomly. It is a white rabbit the same size as others. However, it has horizontal red eyes and displays the name "The Killer Bunny." You can find normal white rabbits with vertical red eyes, but these aren't hostile. The Killer Bunny is hostile to players and all wolves, but will attack players first before wolves. If it spots you within a 15-block radius, it will leap straight toward you.

KILLER BUNNY STATS

Mob Type: Hostile

Health: 10 ♥♥♥♥♥

Attack Strength:

Easy — 5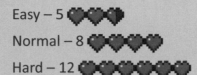

Normal — 8

Hard — 12

Experience: 1–3

Drops: 0–1 raw rabbit, 0–1 rabbit hide, (less commonly) rabbit's foot

Spawn: Killer Bunnies have a one in a thousand chance of spawning instead of a normal rabbit. Like rabbits, they'll spawn in the savannah, plains, swamp, extreme hills, birch forest, and other forested biomes.

Sword Strikes to Kill:

Wood: 2

Stone: 2

Iron: 2

Gold: 2

Diamond: 2

Bow Strikes to Kill: 1–2

Fighting the Killer Bunny

If the Killer Bunny takes you by surprise, it can really knock you back and deal you a hard blow. However, it is pretty easy to kill: just two swipes of any sword should do it.

CHAPTER 20

MAGMA CUBE

Magma cubes are a square 2x2 mob that bounce. They have dark red and black skin and yellow and red eyes. Their accordion-like body expands as they hop up and retracts when they hit the ground.

MAGMA CUBE STATS

Mob Type: Hostile, Nether

Health*:

Large – 16 pts ♥♥♥♥♥♥♥♥

Medium – 4 ♥♥

Tiny – 1 ♥

*Magma cubes also have hidden armor points, which protect them against up to nearly 50 percent of the damage you cause. This means their health, in practice, is higher than the number of hearts they have, and it will take more strikes to kill them.

Attack Strength:

Large – 6 ♥♥♥

Medium – 4 ♥♥

Tiny – 3 ♥♥

Drops: 0–1 magma cream (only medium and large magma cubes drop these)

Spawn: In the Nether.

Sword Strikes to Kill (Large):

Wood: 4

Stone: 3

Iron: 3

Gold: 4

Diamond: 2

Bow Strikes to Kill: 2

Fighting the Magma Cube

The most difficult thing about fighting mobs in the Nether is your location. There are cliffs of Netherrack with dangerous and life-threatening drops, and lava seas, pools, and dripping columns are everywhere. Half the battle is making sure you are somewhere relatively safe and aren't backing up to a drop into lava. You can increase your chances by using Fire Protection enchantments on your armor and Feather Falling on your boots.

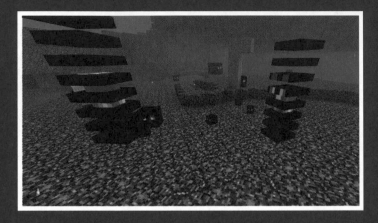

Magma cubes jumping.

Magma cubes are similar to their Overworld cousins, slimes. If you kill a large cube, it spawns 4 medium-sized ones. And when you kill a medium-sized cube, it spawns four tiny cubes. If you are using a diamond sword on a large magma cube, it won't take long to kill. However, if you don't have a diamond sword, an iron sword with Knockback enchantment is a very good alternative. The cube keeps bouncing toward you, and it damages you if it lands on top of you. Knockback helps propel the cube backward so it can't land on you. If it is jumping over you, you still have a chance to stab it with your sword while it is over you. Magma cubes are slow enough that you can take them out with a bow and arrow. The smaller cubes move slowly and have low enough health that it isn't too hard to exterminate them pretty quickly.

CHAPTER 21

SILVERFISH

The silverfish lives in strongholds and in stone blocks in the extreme hills biome. It's one of Minecraft's smallest mobs, taking up less space than a block. However, a silverfish can jump 1 block high and can push a player. It will scurry with a wiggling motion straight to you and inflict 1 point of damage when it touches or pushes you. That's not so bad, compared to other hostile mobs. However, if you attack a silverfish directly, with a weapon, other silverfish nearby (within about 10 blocks) may be woken up and come to join the first silverfish in attacking you back. A silverfish can also disappear into another stone block, making it into a monster egg.

Silverfish will suffocate if they are on a patch of soul sand that is too big (around 5x5 blocks or larger) for them to hustle off. If they are on just one block of soul sand, they can usually get off the block before they die.

SILVERFISH STATS

Mob Type: Hostile, Local

Health: 8 ♥♥♥♥

Attack Strength: 1 ♥

Experience: 5

Drops: None

Spawn: From silverfish spawners in strongholds and in monster eggs (also called silverfish stone) in extreme hills biomes. With a spawner, silverfish can spawn on stone blocks at any light level, but on non-stone blocks only at light level 11 or lower. They can't spawn within 5 blocks of a player.

Sword Strikes to Kill:

Wood: 2

Stone: 2

Iron: 2

Gold: 2

Diamond: 1

Bow Strikes to Kill: 1

Fighting the Silverfish

In general, the silverfish's low health and mild attack strength make it easy to kill quickly. If you kill a silverfish in one hit, which you can do with a diamond sword, it won't awaken the other silverfish hiding in monster eggs nearby. You can also enchant a diamond or iron pickaxe with Sharpness, so that it gives 8 or more attack damage, and use that for mining in extreme hills. That way, when a silverfish emerges, you can give it one swing with your pickaxe and continue mining.

One silverfish is easy to kill, but a swarm can overtake you.

If you don't have a diamond sword or enchanted pickaxe, use an indirect way to kill the silverfish, so that it doesn't wake up other silverfish. Jump on a short pillar of gravel (2 high), and drop lava or gravel on it. To suffocate the silverfish with gravel, you do have to place the gravel against a wall or pillar block so that it can slide down directly on top the silverfish. The silverfish gives a nice, long death squeal when you do this! However, because you need to place the gravel carefully so that it suffocates the silverfish, the better solution is a bucket of lava. You can also use flint and steel very handily to set a single silverfish ablaze. It will die without awakening others.

Although one silverfish by itself is not very harmful, a swarm of silverfish can quickly kill you. If you awaken a swarm of silverfish, you will definitely want to pillar up so that they cannot get to you. When you are mining in extreme hills, make sure you have a short stack of gravel on hand and a bucket of lava.

Whatever you do, don't attack the silverfish with a splash potion, especially a splash Potion of Poison. A Potion of Poison makes multiple "attacks," and with each attack, more silverfish are alerted and you could end up with a very large swarm. A Potion of Harming gives an instant effect so you can kill one silverfish with one splash. However, if there are several silverfish present, some may not be killed by the splash and are then able to summon others.

Mining Monster Eggs

Monster eggs can look like any of the stone blocks: cobblestone, stone, stone brick, cracked stone bricks, mossy stone bricks, or chiseled stone. In an extreme hills biome, they'll appear as stone. However, monster eggs take noticeably longer to mine with a pickaxe than a regular stone block. Once you've mined a few, you'll be able to tell while you are striking a stone block if it is a monster egg. (If you use your hands, monster eggs are actually faster to mine than stone.) When you've woken a silverfish from its egg, a little white cloud appears that looks like the cloud that forms when you kill a mob.

CHAPTER 22

SKELETON

The skelly is one of the big four—the four common mobs of the Minecraft Overworld (the others are the zombie, the spider, and the Creeper) that you'll see daily. When a skeleton is near, you will hear the tinkly sound of bones rattling together.

Although skeletons spawn with a bow, some are able to pick up weapons. If they pick up a more damaging sword, they'll use that instead. Some skeletons spawn with armor or enchanted bows, which will make them harder to kill.

If they are within 16 blocks of you, they will chase you; when they are within 8 blocks of you, they'll start shooting their bows. If you get 16 blocks away from them again, they'll lose interest in you.

As of the Minecraft 1.8 Bountiful Update, skeletons are afraid of wolves (as they should be!). All wolves now chase and attack skeletons without provocation, and the skeleton will run away when it sees a wolf. They will also now run away from a Creeper that is gearing up to explode.

SKELETON STATS

Mob Type: Hostile, Darkness

Health: 20 ♥♥♥♥♥♥♥♥♥♥

Attack Strength (Bow):

Easy – 1 ♥

Normal – 2 ♥

Hard – 4 ♥♥

Attack Strength (Sword):

Easy – 2 ♥

Normal – 2 ♥

Hard – 3 ♥♥

Experience: 5

Drops: 0–2 arrows, more rarely bows and armor (which may be enchanted, but usually badly damaged), 1 skeleton skull (if killed by a charged Creeper)

Spawn: In Overworld at light levels 7 and below, and by skeleton spawners found in dungeons. Also spawns more rarely in the Nether, near Nether fortresses.

Sword Strikes to Kill:

Wood: 4

Stone: 4

Iron: 3

Gold: 4

Diamond: 3

Bow Strikes to Kill: 2

Fighting the Skeleton

When a skeleton attacks you, it fires its arrows more rapidly the closer it gets. With the knockback of an arrow hit from it, you'll find it is difficult to get close enough to use a sword, and you can be hit multiple times while you're trying to do so. To avoid being hit by the skeleton, strafe. Use your left and right move keys (A and D) to move left and right. The one thing you don't want to do with a skeleton is knock it back by sprinting and striking it with your sword. This knock back actually gives the skeleton more time to charge and fire its bow.

If you are mining in a cave and you've captured a skeleton's attention, draw it to a location where there are some blocks you can hide behind. When it starts coming around the corner of the block, attack the edge of it before it fully emerges. As with other mob attacks, use the blocking technique to limit the damage the skeleton does.

Skeletons and other mobs are more likely to spawn with armor, weapons, and enchantments in Hard difficulty or when it is a full moon.

Skeletons burn in the daylight, unless they are wearing a helmet or a pumpkin (or are in water), so one passive tactic is to try to draw them out into the open during the day. Once they've taken some damage, finish them off with your sword or bow so you can reap the rewards of dropped loot.

Skeletons are not solid, which leads to an interesting scenario. If you are close to one, and its back is against a wall, walk right up into the block it is standing in. You are now inside the skeleton and can hit it with your sword. Meanwhile, all the skelly can do is fire its arrows meaninglessly into the ground. Score!

CHAPTER 23

SLIME

The slime is a large (2x2x2 blocks) cubed mob. It's green, very slightly transparent, and makes a squelchy sound as it hops straight toward you. When you kill the large slime, it breaks into up to four smaller ones. These split into up to four tiny ones when you kill them.

There are two good things about slimes. One, they're not too fast and not too strong, so they're not difficult to kill. Second, they provide slimeballs as a drop, which you can use to make magma cream, leads to tie animals to posts, sticky pistons, and slime blocks you can bounce on.

Slimes are actually relatively rare. In swamps, they will only spawn at night where the light is 7 or below. The moon also affects when they spawn. They spawn more during a full moon and not at all during a new moon. They can also spawn at any light levels at lower depths of the world (levels 0–39), but only under special conditions and in 1 of about 10 chunks. A chunk is a segment of the Minecraft world that is 16 blocks square and the full height of the world, 256 blocks. Chunks are used in the programming code to manage mobs spawning and despawning and rendering, among other things.

SLIME STATS

Mob Type: Hostile, Local

Health:

> Big – 16 ❤❤❤❤❤❤❤❤
>
> Small – 4 ❤❤
>
> Tiny – 1 ❤

Attack Strength:

> Big – 4 pts ❤❤
>
> Small – 2 pts ❤
>
> Tiny – 0

Experience:

> Big – 4
>
> Small – 2
>
> Tiny – 1

Drops: 0–2 slimeballs, from tiny slime

Spawn: Swamps in low light and in levels below 40.

Sword Strikes to Kill (Big Slime):

> Wood: 4
>
> Stone: 3

Iron: 3

Gold: 4

Diamond: 2

Bow Strikes to Kill: 2

Fighting the Slime

Slimes are not very difficult to kill. Use your sword and click fast. Although the smaller slimes will seem like they can overtake you, they are very easy to kill. You can punch a tiny slime with your fist and it will die and give you a slimeball for your effort. Overall, they are mostly just a hindrance, especially if you are mining and come across a slime-generating chunk. When you do, block off your mining corridors to leave just one-block gaps that only the smaller slimes can get through.

Killing a large or medium slime will spawn up to four additional smaller slimes.

CHAPTER 24

SPIDERS AND SPIDER JOCKEYS

ou can always tell when a spider is nearby because of its typical scratchy hiss. (If you can hear one but can't see it, it's probably just overhead, in a tree or on your roof.) Spiders are neutral at higher, daylight levels of light. In the dark, at light levels of 7 and below, they become hostile. And once hostile, they never revert back to neutral.

Spiders are very agile, and they can move quickly and jump across a 3- or 4-block gap. They can also climb up vertical blocks, as if the blocks had ladders attached. Spiders are two blocks wide, so they can't fit through 1x1 gaps. They do fit through 1 high x 2 wide spaces, though.

Before the latest 1.8 Bountiful Update, spiders could see and track you through walls. With 1.8, they can no longer do this.

If you are playing on Hard mode, spiders can sometimes spawn with a status effect. A status effect is a special ability, usually delivered through a potion. Spiders in Hard mode can spawn with Invisibility, Regeneration, Strength, or Swiftness effects that are pretty much permanent.

SPIDER STATS

Type: Neutral (Hostile at low light levels)

Health: 16 ♥♥♥♥♥♥♥♥

Attack strength:

Easy – 2 ♥

Normal – 2 ♥

Hard – 3 ♥♥

Experience: 5

Drops: 0–2 string, 0–1 spider eye

Spawn: In the Overworld, in light levels of 7 or less, and in dungeons from spider spawners.

Sword Strikes to Kill:

Wood: 4

Stone: 3

Iron: 3

Gold: 4

Diamond: 2

Bow Strikes to Kill: 2

Fighting the Spider

Because spiders are fast, the best way to kill them is with a bow and arrow, if you have the chance. If you must use a sword, first try to make sure you are on higher ground than the spider. If the spider is above you, it can jump on top of you and cause extra damage. If you can't get to higher ground, move to a flatter area so that the spider at least isn't above you.

You can also use flint and steel to set a spider alight. Make sure you are a couple blocks away so you don't catch on fire also! For extra power against the spider, enchant your sword with the Bane of Arthropods enchantment, as this will deliver extra damage to spiders. If you are doing well with experience levels and can enchant extra swords, you can enchant one sword to use while mining.

You can also use the width of the spider to your advantage to slip through a 1-block wide gap and attack the spider through the gap. Overall, the spider has lower health than the other four common mobs (zombie, skeleton, and Creeper, which all have 20 points of health), so it is a bit easier to defeat.

Beware the Spider Jockey

Very rarely, a spider will spawn with a skeleton riding on its shoulders. About 1 in 100 spiders spawn this way. This hybrid monster is called a spider jockey and is a deadly combination. It carries all the attack strength of both a spider and skeleton put together. It has the climbing ability of a spider and the accurate aim of the skeleton. However, you will have to kill each one of them separately, and each will provide its separate drops: arrows and bones or string and spider eyes.

Ideally, when you spot a spider jockey, you will run away and hide, so as to preserve your life. If you have enchanted weaponry and armor though, or are confident in your combat skills, you can be bolder. Use your bow and arrow, first to kill the skeleton on top and then the spider.

About 1 in 100 spiders spawn with a skeleton rider.

CHAPTER 25

WITCH

Witches look a lot like villagers, except for their tall black hats, purple cloaks, and grayish skin. Their noses are big like a villager's, but a witch's nose can wiggle and has one large wart on it. Despite their good looks and charm, witches are one of the most harmful mobs you encounter in the Overworld on a normal day. If you are low on health, it might be best to avoid them, as they are difficult to kill and can inflict a lot of damage. They are difficult to kill because they heal themselves while you are fighting them. They use helpful potions on themselves and throw harmful potions at you.

When witches were first introduced in the game, they only spawned in witch huts. Witch huts are small wooden homes raised above the water in swamps. A witch still spawns with a witch hut, but they can also spawn anywhere in the Overworld where there is a light level 7 or below, so you may find one in your spelunking expeditions. And if a villager is struck by lightning, it turns into a witch.

WITCH STATS

Mob Type: Hostile, Local

Health: 26 ♥♥♥♥♥♥♥♥♥♥♥♥♥

Attack Strength: Witches attack you through potions, and two will cause damage to your health (the Potion of Poison and Potion of Harming). One potion of poison can cause up 38 or more points of damage but will always leave you with 1 point of health, so it won't kill you. A Potion of Harming can cause up to 12 points of health.

Experience: 5

Drops: 0–6 sticks, 0–6 gunpowder, 0–6 sugar, 0–6 spider eyes, 0–6 glowstone dust, 0–6 redstone, 0–6 glass bottles, (more rarely) 1 potion (Healing, Fire Resistance, Swiftness, or Water Breathing)

Spawn: In the Overworld at light levels 7 or less and witch huts in the Swamp biome. With the 1.8 Minecraft Bountiful Update, villagers who are struck by lightning will turn into witches.

Sword Strikes to Kill:

🗡 Wood: 6

🗡 Stone: 5

Iron: 4

Gold: 6

Diamond: 4

Bow Strikes to Kill: 3

Fighting the Witch

There is a logic to what potions witches will throw at you and when. When you are within 8 blocks of a witch, it will throw a Potion of Slowness at you to slow you down, unless you already are under a Slowness status effect. If you don't retreat, and your health is 8 points or over, they'll throw a Potion of Poison at you. Poison won't kill you, but it can take you down to a single point of health (half a heart). Then, if you get within 3 blocks of a witch, they sometimes throw a Potion of Weakness, as long as you aren't already inflicted with a Weakness effect. Finally, once you have been inflicted by Slowness and Poison, they'll start throwing Potions of Harming. These can and will kill you.

Meanwhile, as soon as the witch sees you, the witch drinks potions to heal itself. They'll guzzle a Potion of Healing when they're damaged and a Potion of Fire Resistance if they're on fire. If they're underwater, they can drink a Potion of Water Breathing. Also, if they are 12 or so blocks away from you, they can drink a Potion of Swiftness so they can quickly get close to you before they attack.

This witch has just drunk a Potion of Healing and thrown a Potion of Slowness.

The best way to fight a witch is to use your bow and arrow from a distance. The bow has a longer range than a witch throwing splash potions, so you can come out of the battle completely unscathed. If long range is not an option, your best bet is to rush the witch immediately. If you can, surprise them by keeping hidden as long as possible. Get in as many strikes with your sword as you can before they start drinking their Potion of Healing. (You can tell they're drinking their potion by the bubbles floating up from them.) You can kill a witch quickly with fast swordplay before they even get around to throwing the Potion of Harming.

When you do kill them, they'll drop materials from potion making, sometimes a stick (perhaps from their unseen broomstick?) and, more rarely, a potion that they were about to drink.

CHAPTER 26

THE WITHER

The Wither is an extremely powerful boss mob. It is the only hostile mob in the Minecraft game that the player creates. To create a Wither, you must have been to the Nether to collect soul sand and three wither skeleton skulls. You arrange the soul sand blocks in a T-shape and then place the skulls on the top three blocks. When the last skull is placed, the blocks turn into the Wither boss mob. You must place one skull as the last block or the Wither won't spawn.

The spawning of the Wither is a dramatic event. The sky turns slightly darker, and the Wither flashes blue. It grows larger and larger, gaining health. (Like the other boss mob, the Ender Dragon, the Wither's health bar will show on your screen.) During this period, it is immune to any attacks. Finally, when its full health is reached, the Wither flashes and creates a giant explosion around itself and changes into its final, somewhat larger form. A black, flying, skeleton-like, three-headed, projectile-hurling hostile form. The Wither immediately and constantly attacks any living entities it sees—you, a cow, everything—flying from target to target. The projectiles it hurls are Wither skulls. There are two types of Wither skull it can throw: fast black ones and slower, rarer blue skulls. Both have the same explosive power as Ghast fireballs. The black skulls can't explode hard blocks like cobblestone, while the blue skulls can break all blocks except for bedrock and the End portal frame. So the Wither causes a lot of destruction—to the world around you and to you.

THE WITHER STATS

Mob Type: Boss

Health: 300 ♥♥♥♥♥♥♥♥♥♥ x 15

Armor Points: 4 🛡🛡

Attack Strength:

Easy – 5 ♥♥♥

Normal – 8 ♥♥♥♥

Hard – 12 ♥♥♥♥♥♥

(On Normal and Hard, the Wither attack also gives Wither effect, which is similar to poison.)

Experience: 50

Drops: 1 Nether star

Spawn: Initiated by player.

Sword Strikes to Kill:

⚔ Wood: 60

⚔ Stone: 50

Iron: 43

Gold: 60

Diamond: 38

Bow Strikes to Kill: 34

Fighting the Wither

There are quite a few reasons not to create and fight the Wither. (1) The Wither has 100 more points of health than the Ender Dragon. (2) It can throw three Wither skulls at a time, some of which can destroy any blocks except bedrock. (3) Besides blast damage, Wither skulls also inflict the Wither effect on you. This drains your health and also makes it difficult to see what your health is because it turns your health bar black. (4) Inflicting the Wither effect on you actually heals the Wither by 5 points. (5) It is immune to fire and lava. (6) If you get the Wither down to half health, it suddenly gets Wither armor protection, which makes it immune to arrows. (It can't fly at this point, which is a plus.) (7) The only potion you can use against a Wither is the Potion of Healing, as it is an undead mob.

There are two reasons to fight the Wither yourself: (1) for the bragging rights and (2) for the ultra rare drop, a single Nether star. Killing the Wither is the only way to get a Nether star, and a Nether star is the key ingredient for creating beacons. Beacons are made of glass, Nether star, and obsidian. In addition to making a powerful light beam, if you place a beacon on a pyramid of iron, diamond, emerald, or gold, you can give yourself and anyone nearby the beacon special status effect powers.

To take on the Wither, you must have enchanted armor and weapons. You won't survive without it, and you'll pretty likely die even with it. You can make it much easier on yourself if you go to the End and defeat the Ender Dragon first. Then you can go back to the End to stage your Wither battle there. In the End, the Wither will also attack Endermen, who will join in the fight. They will help you get the Wither to half health, when at least it can't fly any more.

Regardless, you will want to stage your battle away from your home base, to protect it from the massive explosive destruction that will be caused. Enlist any help you can, from other players on multiplayer servers or by building iron golems. Use obsidian to create a safe area, and to protect the extra armor, weapons, and potions you will need. If possible, create a special space, walled with obsidian, to confine your battle and reduce unnecessary amounts of flying about and chasing.

The Wither firing an explosive skull at you.

Your bow should be enchanted with the highest Power and Punch level you can afford, as well as Infinity. Your sword, also, should be enchanted with the highest Smite level, along with Knockback. (Looting won't help deliver more Nether stars.) In addition, brew multiple bottles of Potion of Healing, both for yourself and to harm the Wither, along with several Golden Apples, and some Potions of Strength, Regeneration, and Swiftness. For your armor, get the highest level of Blast Protection, if you can. Before your battle, eat an enchanted apple and drink your Strength, Swiftness, and Regen potions. Use your bow for the first half of the battle, then when the Wither is no longer flying, use your sword. Good luck!

CHAPTER 27
WITHER SKELETON

Wither skeletons look similar to regular Overworld skeletons, but they are 2.5 blocks high instead of 2. Their bones are a dark grayish black. They only spawn in the Nether, in or by Nether fortresses. The mouth of a Wither skeleton is not as wide as a regular skeleton. Whereas skeletons are equipped with a bow, the Wither skeleton carries a stone sword. Like skeletons, Wither skeletons will run away from wolves and can pick up armor and weapons. Unlike Overworld skeletons, they won't burn in daylight. They will flash with fire for a moment, but they aren't killed or damaged. They aren't damaged at all by either lava or fire, because they are natives of the Hell biome of the Nether.

Wither skeletons strike you with their sword, which gives you the Wither effect, similar to poisoning. The Wither effect lasts

10 seconds and gives 1 point of damage every couple of seconds. When you've received the Wither effect, your health bar turns black. You can heal yourself with milk, potions, and the like. Wither skeleton attacks will knock you back, so be especially careful if you are near cliffs or ledges. Also beware if one picks up a bow, as it will use the bow, and the arrows will be on fire.

WITHER SKELETON STATS

Mob Type: Hostile, Nether, Local

Health: 20 ♥♥♥♥♥♥♥♥♥♥

Attack Strength:

Easy – 4 ♥♥

Normal – 7 ♥♥♥♥

Hard – 10 ♥♥♥♥♥

Experience: 5

Drops: 0–1 coal, 0–2 bones, (more rarely) a stone sword or 1 Wither skeleton skull, used to create a Wither boss. A Wither skeleton is more likely to drop a skull if it's killed by a charged creeper.

Spawn: In or near Nether fortresses at light level 7 or lower.

Sword Strikes to Kill:

⚔ Wood: 4

⚔ Stone: 4

⚔ Iron: 3

⚔ Gold: 4

⚔ Diamond: 3

Wither skeletons move fast. They walk as fast as a player and also can sprint. And because they can deal a fairly large amount of damage to you, it is best to be prepared and plan safe places or escape routes, especially if you are visiting the Nether without powerfully enchanted weapons and armor. For example, because Wither skeletons can't pass through 2-high blocks, you can place blocks on fortress corridor ceilings to prevent them from following you. Have Potions of Healing or Regeneration at the ready.

First, at a distance (12 blocks or so), use a bow enchanted with Power as well as Punch. Punch will knock back the target, which can buy you some more time. Closer to the skeleton, use your sword. Once you are close, though, it is highly likely that this mob will give you the Wither effect. You'll want to keep a melee as short as possible, so use a diamond sword enchanted with Sharpness or Smite. The Smite enchantment is even more damaging to undead mobs than the Sharpness enchantment, so if you can spare an extra sword to use just against the undead, do so. (However, you'll often find Blazes and Wither skeletons nearby or together, and the Smite enchantment doesn't work against blazes.)

That said, the most powerful enchantment for damaging your enemy is Smite V or Sharpness V. A diamond sword with either of these will kill a Wither skeleton in one strike. With Smite IV or with Sharpness IV, you'll need just two strokes to kill it. Because Wither skeleton skulls are rare and essential for creating a Wither, try to use a Looting enchanted sword to improve your chances of getting a skull.

If you can't kill the Wither skeleton in one stroke, retreat to or make a 2-high block that it can't enter. Draw it near you, attack with your sword, then quickly move back into your safe zone out of range of their sword. Heal if you need to, and repeat.

A Wither skeleton standing next to its cousin, the regular skeleton.

CHAPTER 28

WOLF

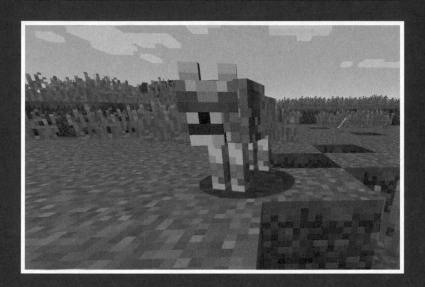

A wolf can exist in three states: wild, tamed, and hostile. A wild wolf is grayish and its tail droops down. A hostile wolf has red eyes and makes snarling or growling sounds. A tamed wolf has lighter fur, its tail angles up, and it has a collar.

Wild wolves are neutral and won't attack you. They live in small groups, or packs, and attack sheep and rabbits. All wolves, including tame ones, will also attack skeletons without being attacked first by them. However, if you attack a wild wolf, all wild wolves nearby will turn hostile and attack you. They will continue to be hostile and attack you until you die. A tamed wolf never becomes hostile to players.

WOLF STATS

Mob Type: Neutral

Health:

Wild – 8

Tame – 20

Attack Strength (Wild):

Easy – 3

Normal – 4

Hard – 6

Attack Strength (Tamed): 4

Experience: 1–3

Drops: None

Spawn: In Forest and Taiga biomes.

Sword Strikes to Kill (Wild):

Wood: 2

Stone: 2

Iron: 2

Gold: 2

Diamond: 1

Bow Strikes to Kill (Wild): 1

A hostile wolf's tail sticks straight out and it has red eyes, an unprovoked wild wolf's tail points down, and a healthy tamed wolf's tail points up.

Fighting the Wolf

It's much smarter to never attack a wolf, because wolves remain hostile and they attack as a group. If, for some reason, you have inadvertently damaged a wolf and a pack is now after you, your best tactic is to escape. If you can, tunnel away and make sure to close off your tunnel's entrance! You'll need torches to light your way, of course. A hostile mob has a chance of despawning or disappearing from the game if it isn't within 32 blocks of a player for more than half a minute. They will definitely despawn if they are more than 128 blocks from a player. So tunnel away for at least 128 blocks before you come out.

CHAPTER 29

ZOMBIE

It's hard to make it through a night without seeing a zombie or a morning without seeing a zombie go up in flames. If you see one alight, strike it fast for a final death blow so you can get the XP.

Zombies are the most common hostile mob in Minecraft. In case you haven't noticed, the zombies look a bit like Steve with a turquoise T-shirt and blue pants. (There's a story in there somewhere!)

Some zombies spawn as zombie villagers, which have the same face as a villager, just green. And if a zombie attacks a villager, it will turn the villager into a zombie villager. There's also another type of zombie, the baby zombie, which you can read about in the baby zombie chapter.

ZOMBIE STATS

Mob type: Hostile, Darkness

Health: 20 ♥♥♥♥♥♥♥♥♥♥

Attack Strength:

Easy – 2 ♥

Normal – 4 ♥♥

Hard – 5 ♥♥♥

Experience: 5

Drops: 0–2 rotten flesh, (more rarely) a carrot, iron ingot, potato, armor and weapons (if they holding them), a zombie head (if they are killed by a charged creeper)

Spawn: In Overworld in light levels of 7 or lower.

Sword Strikes to Kill:

Wood: 4

Stone: 4

Iron: 3

Gold: 4

Diamond: 3

Bow Strikes to Kill: 3

Fighting the Zombie

If you don't want to fight a zombie, just draw it into sunlight (if its day and you're not in a cave!). However, of all the common mobs, zombies are probably the easiest to defeat. They let you know pretty clearly when they're nearby with some good loud groans, and they move pretty slowly. If there's water between you and the zombie, it will take forever to get to you! And as you know, they will burn and die in sunlight (unless they are in water), making them a darkness-only pest.

A villager zombie burning up in the sun.

Zombies can spawn with armor, an iron shovel, or an iron sword. They can also pick up and wear armor, including mob heads dropped by a charged Creeper killing another zombie, skeleton, or Creeper. (This means you could find a zombie wearing a creeper head!) In any case, with armor, zombies become more difficult to kill, and while wearing a helmet they will not burn in the sun. Also, if you are playing on Hard mode, injuring one zombie will cause others to come help attack you.

A zombie with an enchanted shovel!

Use a bow and arrow to kill a zombie from a distance and you'll suffer no damage, as they can only attack you at close range. Face to face, you should be able to knock a zombie out with your sword pretty easily; a sword enchanted with Knockback can also help.

CHAPTER 30

ZOMBIE PIGMAN

The zombie pigman is a very common mob in the Nether, but they are neutral. This means that if you ignore them, they will ignore you. And that is usually the best course of action. You can occasionally find them in the Overworld, as they can spawn near Nether portals. In the very rare chance that an Overworld pig is struck by lightning, it will turn into a zombie pigman, though without a sword.

ZOMBIE PIGMAN STATS

Mob Type: Neutral, Nether

Health: 20 ♥♥♥♥♥♥♥♥♥♥

Attack Strength:

Easy – 5

Normal – 9

Hard – 13

Experience: 5

Drops: 0–2 Rotten flesh, 0–1 gold nuggets, (more rarely) gold swords and gold ingots

Spawn: In the Nether at any light level and in the Overworld by a Nether portal or when lightning strikes close to a pig.

Sword Strikes to Kill*:

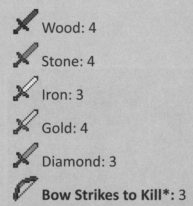

Wood: 4

Stone: 4

Iron: 3

Gold: 4

Diamond: 3

Bow Strikes to Kill*: 3

*The zombie pigman also has 2 armor points, which means you will need more strikes to kill it.

Fighting the Zombie Pigman

As with all neutral mobs, it's better to avoid fighting with zombie pigmen. Any zombie pigman within 32 blocks of you (after you've attacked one of their kind) will be provoked, and if you get within 16 blocks they will chase and attack you. The only way to escape is to sprint (if you have a clear escape route), use a Potion of Swiftness, or ride away on a horse. If you must, try to use a bow from far away, so swarms won't attack you. If you've inadvertently struck one, and there are others about, try to dig into Netherrack and down a little bit. Close the gap behind you, but leave a 1-block high gap at the pigman's foot level. This should allow you to hack away at their feet, killing them. When the mob stops coming for you, or when you get tired of killing them, tunnel 128 blocks away in one direction to despawn them. When you return, new pigmen who know nothing about the fight will spawn and leave you alone.

If you attack one zombie pigman, all the pigmen nearby will come in a horde to attack you.